Participatory Culture

Participatory Culture

Interviews

Henry Jenkins

polity

The right of Henry Jenkins to be identified as Author of this Work has been asserted in accordance with the UK Copyright, Designs and Patents Act 1988.

First published in 2019 by Polity Press

Polity Press
65 Bridge Street
Cambridge CB2 1UR, UK

Polity Press
101 Station Landing
Suite 300
Medford, MA 02155, USA

ISBN-13: 978-1-5095-3845-4
ISBN-13: 978-1-5095-3846-1(pb)

A catalog record for this book is available from the British Library.

Library of Congress Cataloging-in-Publication Date
Names: Jenkins, Henry, 1958- author.
Title: Participatory culture : interviews / Henry Jenkins.
Description: Cambridge, UK ; Medford, MA : Polity Press, [2019] | Includes
    bibliographical references and index.
Identifiers: LCCN 2019005171 (print) | LCCN 2019007502 (ebook) | ISBN
    9781509538478 (Epub) | ISBN 9781509538454 (hardback) | ISBN 9781509538461
    (pbk.)
Subjects: LCSH: Mass media and culture. | Mass media--Social aspects. |
    Social change.
Classification: LCC P94.6 (ebook) | LCC P94.6 .J459 2019 (print) | DDC
    302.23--dc23
LC record available at https://lccn.loc.gov/2019005171

Typeset in 10 on 14pt Utopia
by Fakenham Prepress Solutions, Fakenham, Norfolk NR21 8NL
Printed and bound in Great Britain by TJ Internationsl Limited

For further information on Polity, visit our website:
politybooks.com

Contents

CONTENTS

Introduction: Between Blog and Book

My last book for Polity Press – *Participatory Culture in a Networked Era* – was an extended conversation with two of my best thinking partners, danah boyd and Mizuko Ito. Over the course of the book, we tackled some shared concerns:

- In what sense do we believe contemporary culture is more participatory than what came before?
- Who gets to participate and who is left outside this collective exchange?
- Why is participation a good thing?
- How have ideas about the value of participation and connection impacted the way learning takes place inside and outside the classroom?
- How have new business models and technological infrastructures emerged which encourage and profit from social media engagements and grassroots media-making?
- What does activism look like in a world where the ability to create and circulate media at a grassroots level is widely distributed?
- What roles should intellectuals play in promoting greater participation in culture, education, and politics?

Participatory Culture: Interviews is intended as a companion to that other book, picking up on many of these same issues, but broadening the conversation to incorporate more diverse thinkers whose work has informed my own perspective. You do not need to have read the other book to find something of value here, but it would certainly help to provide the larger contexts in which these exchanges took place. In both cases, the structures of the book are intended to suggest that dialogic writing – that is, exchanges between multiple thinkers – is a more appropriate way to align form with content here, to create a mode of academic writing that is consistent with the values of a more participatory culture.

Since its launch in June 2006, I have made more than 2,000 posts to my blog, *Confessions of an Aca-Fan* (*henryjenkins.org*), including interviews, dialogs, and conversations with more than 350 other scholars, journalists, educators, artists, activists, and public intellectuals. This book contains a baker's dozen of my favorite interviews with people whom I regard as important mentors and thinking partners. (Narrowing down to this small number of selections was painful, so I am putting a list of other related interviews at the end of each section of my introductions so you can dig deeper into these issues.)

While I began this blog as a means of promoting my own ideas and activities, it has more and more become a platform for prompting and hosting exchanges that advance the field of cultural and media studies. I am interested in how to create dialogic and collaborative spaces within academia, including spaces where academics can engage with and learn from conversations with practitioners of all kinds, where academic exchanges may bridge disciplinary and national borders, and where we might hammer out disagreements as opposed to lobbing peer-reviewed journal articles over the wall every few years.

Amongst those many interviews, there are many possible books I could have curated – some more focused than this one around the creative industries and their output, say, or around the study of fandom, or around comics and other popular media, or around transmedia storytelling practices, all important dimensions of my scholarship and teaching. Building on the earlier book, I have structured this collection around three core concepts – participatory culture, participatory learning, and participatory politics.

We will explore each of these concepts in more depth as the book progresses, but, for now, we can define these concepts in the following way:

Participatory culture refers to a culture in which large numbers of people from all walks of life have the capacity to produce and share media with each other, often responding critically to the products of mass media, and often circulating what they create fluidly across a range of different niche publics.

Participatory learning refers to pedagogical approaches that are modeled after the logics and practices of participatory culture, including those which incorporate games, social media, fandom, and mobile technologies into the learning process. Mimi Ito describes such practices as connected learning and, while there are some differences between the two, I find her model a compelling way to address opportunities and risks, and, in particular, inequalities of access to opportunities to learn through participation.

Participatory politics refers to what happens when a generation of young people who have grown up with more opportunities to meaningfully participate in culture turns its voices to struggles for social justice and political change. Participatory politics may include engagement with electoral and institutional politics, but it may also be directed towards shaping the world through informing public opinion or directing pressure against corporate interests.

Taken together, these interviews trace the ways our collective understanding of these concepts evolved over time. Moreover, I hope that reading these assembled interviews will allow us to reflect upon knowledge-production as a conversation amongst people who learn by listening to and building upon each other's insights. To further aid our understanding, I asked each interview subject to share short reflections on how their own thinking has changed as they have dug deeper into their scholarship or simply responded to changing times. These statements, almost without exception, speak to a sense of crisis as our contemporary culture has failed to achieve the democratic potentials we once anticipated as a consequence of the participatory turn.

Long before I launched my own blog, I was interested in the ways that blogging might illustrate the nature of participatory culture. Writing about blogging in *Technology Review* (2001), I argued that we might trace two distinct but interlocking accounts of media history:

- first, the history of commercial media production and circulation, including the history of the publishing, advertising, journalism, and entertainment industries;
- second, the history of grassroots media production and circulation – the history of toy printing presses and zines, Super 8 movies, and fan fiction.

Such an approach does not see participatory culture springing full-born over night with the widespread embrace of digital and mobile technologies. Rather, digital culture provides resources that respond to several hundred years of struggle by grassroots communities wishing for better means of shaping the national agenda and sharing their stories with each other. We might, for example, point to the ways that the counterculture of the 1960s sought to route around mass media through the use of hyperlocal radio stations, alternative newspapers and newsletters, underground comics, concerts, posters, and street theatre to cite just a few examples. It is striking that many counterculture leaders were among the first to embrace the concept of the virtual community, incorporating digital tools and practices in their long-evolving repertoire.

Understanding the newer forms of participatory culture as part of an older struggle between top-down and bottom-up forms of power is helpful in allowing us to recognize that these struggles are apt to persist for many decades to come. The rise of the digital did not resolve these conflicts but rather shifted the grounds upon which these struggles occurred, allowing for new relationships between the forces struggling over access to communication resources. The outcomes of these struggles are not predictable – other than that no one side is going to finish the other off any time soon. So, at the moment, the situation feels dark, because some of the opportunities we once had to share our ideas are shut down, some are deploying grassroots media to demonize and silence other communities, and those in power have learned new ways to deploy that power in pursuit of their own interests. Yet there have been moments of hope and despair before, and the key thing is to continue to struggle toward a more participatory culture, one which more fully realizes our ideals, and not to give over to narratives of inevitability in which we are either overwhelmed or liberated by technological change.

Understood in these terms, blogging falls at the intersection where grassroots media producers curate and respond to content generated by mass media producers – reframing, say, pieces produced by professional journalists for their own community, often addressing groups that have been underserved by mass media. Today, social media plays many of these same functions, with research showing most young people gain information about current events primarily through content shared by their friends via Facebook, Twitter, Instagram, and other such platforms. Some describe such practices as citizen journalism, a term which troubles me for several reasons. First, I think it is important for professional journalists to recognize that they are also citizens and that their mission takes place in a larger civic context. But, second, what I do with my blog is not intended to be journalism per se, but rather represents an extension of my professorial role, as a means of speaking from within my discipline to a larger informed public which is also confronting and trying to think through a moment of rapid media change.

When I first wrote about blogging in 2001, it was in the wake of the dot.com bust, and the Web 2.0 companies had not yet found ways to profit from our participation: "We're in a lull between waves of commercialization in digital media, and bloggers are seizing the moment, potentially increasing cultural diversity and lowering barriers to cultural participation." Even as I was writing, the survivors of the dot.com crash were regrouping, reformulating lessons learned, and developing new business models that would become known as Web 2.0. These business models spoke of grassroots creativity and collective intelligence – two cornerstones of participatory culture – as what would drive customers to embrace social media platforms that would allow them to share content with each other online. These companies would provide the platform both as a way to drive eyeballs to advertisements and as a means of mining data on their user bases. My critiques of these models surface in both *Participatory Culture in a Networked Era* and *Spreadable Media*. But, in 2001, in a moment of optimism, I saw a dramatic increase in our opportunities to produce and circulate media. If we do not yet live in a fully participatory culture, we clearly live in a more participatory culture as more people – individually and collectively – have embraced those potentials. If my excitement about blogging may now seem quaint, it is because blogging has, to some degree, run its cycle: blogging has become a normative practice, no longer a point of innovation within our rapidly changing society. Academic blogging still represents an important outlet for public intellectuals, but social media took over some of the everyday functions of blogs, and the technological infrastructure supporting the blog community was abandoned by companies seeking the next new thing. Today, podcasting is where the excitement is – a site of rapid growth and widespread experimentation, a space where grassroots cultural production exists alongside a new growth of commercial media. I am also experimenting in this space through my own podcast, done in conjunction with Colin Maclay, the Director of the Annenberg Innovation Lab: *How Do You Like It So Far?*

In another early piece (2002), I contrasted the logics of blogging and culture jamming. The culture jammer seeks to disrupt the flow of mass media, the blogger seeks to redirect it (calling attention often to information that might otherwise be lost or ignored). I wrote, "In some cases, bloggers actively deconstruct pernicious claims or poke fun at other sites; in others, they form temporary tactical alliances with other bloggers or with media producers to insure that important messages get more widely circulated. These bloggers have become important grassroots intermediaries – facilitators, not jammers, of the signal flow." Here, I was thinking about blogging in its earliest forms – as the gathering together and annotation of meaningful links. Yet, blogging, over time, became more than that – a space of reflection and conversation which sought to surface and share perspectives that were often left out of professional media content.

As such, blogging offered enormous opportunities for public intellectuals to translate ideas that were often locked away within academia into language and formats that might allow them to travel more broadly across the culture. I often remind my students that my job title, "Professor," contains within it the ethical obligation to profess – that is, to make information available to anyone who wants to know, to spread ideas more widely across the culture, and to create a context where different thinkers might come together to share knowledge with each other. This is very much how I understand the work of my blog. By virtue of my status within the academic world, I have the capacity to direct attention, to amplify voices.

I also have the opportunity to draw other scholars into conversation with a larger public of readers, which, in the case of my blog, includes fans, educators, industry leaders, creative artists, activists, students, and so forth. I have been experimenting with different ways for academic writing to be more dialogic. My blog sometimes includes guest posts, most often from my students, allowing younger and emerging scholars to share their perspectives. I have organized some large-scale conversations, especially as they relate to the field of fandom studies, where dozens of scholars pair off together, writing back and forth to explore the intersections between their work. I have even exported this model to academic journals in the case of a conversation about participation which I co-hosted with Nick Couldry in the *International Journal of Communication*. I have done one-on-one exchanges myself with important scholars whose work intersects my own, using this format to work through disagreements or clarify and contrast core concepts from our work. And finally, as is illustrated here, I conduct interviews in which I frame a set of questions that I think will be of interest to my readers and wait for the research subjects to respond by email.

When I first discovered blogging, I was fascinated with the speed of communication – watching people live-blog events and instantly spread information out to their public. I described bloggers as the "minute men of the digital revolution," because of their ability to rapidly respond to shifting conditions on the ground and, in effect, spread the alarm to every Middlesex village and farm. As I wrote, "Bloggers are turning the hunting and gathering, sampling and critiquing the rest of us do online into an extreme sport. We surf the web, they snowboard it." As an academic who writes about contemporary culture, I am often frustrated by the slow pace of academic publishing, where it can take years for what I write to appear in print, and as my words are waiting, locked down, unable to be updated, while I watch the world changing around us in ways that may at any moment render these arguments obsolete. I also see people locked into their positions, unable to respond to challenges in real time, unable to think through points of differences and consider alternative perspectives. I see the scholarly blog as trying to find a balance between the immediacy of live blogging and the sluggishness of academic publishing, hoping to produce posts that are timely *and* reflective, which speak to the current moment by linking it to larger historical and theoretical debates.

Because of my interest in the temporality of blogging, you may well ask why I am now collecting some of these blog pieces in a book, or, for that matter, why I am encouraging you to revisit interviews that were conducted, in some cases, 15 years ago. The book has what the blog lacks – a sense of permanence – and, through permanence, we can communicate something else: that some ideas have lasting value, are worth returning to because they contain insights that may withstand the test of time – or, conversely, because they provide a time capsule that future generations may use to better understand how we responded to a period of rapid change. While I tend to read my work in tactical terms – what I write reflects what I can know and say at a particular moment in time – I also think we secure ground over time. Our ideas are tested against new developments and contested through academic dialogue, but, over time, we deepen our understanding of the phenomenon we are trying to describe. Consequently, I have chosen these particular interviews because these people and these exchanges taught me something important, something that has stayed with me.

As we read these interviews in a printed book, we shift temporalities – from the immediate to the long term – but I want to remind you that none of us saw ourselves as speaking beyond the current moment. I was shocked when I first heard that people were assigning my blog posts in classes or citing them in academic articles, because I had seen them as drafts where I think out loud and solicit feedback from others working on the same topics. I did not see these blog pieces as "finished" – not that anything we write is ever finished. Rather, these posts were open and fluid (reflecting the fact that blog technology allows me to go back and correct or change texts after they have been released to the reading public, again creating a very different dynamic than authors' experience working in print).

This is why blogging feels so liberating – words are not precious, ideas are not contained, thoughts are not locked down, and one's immediate reflections, for better or worse, can go out to the world and we do not need anyone's permission or approval. But this means we make a category confusion when we bring print-based assumptions to bear upon blog content. These are ideas in a rawer form than writing which has gone through the editorial or peer-review process, receiving active and collaborative revision before going out to the world.

I am trying to replicate my voice as a blogger here – as if I could speak directly to you, as if there was no gap between reading and writing – though I know how many other people will work upon and pass along these words before they reach your eyes. No matter how much I tell you to read these interviews as if they were posted on a blog, the fact that you are reading them in a book will change the mental frame you bring to them. I can only hope that they will also inspire further conversation and reflection, that you will pass some of these thoughts along through your social media, that you may share them with students and colleagues, or – even better – that you will act upon them to change the world. What happens next, like this book itself, is in your hands.

Further Reading

"Blog This!" (2001) and "Interactive Audiences? The 'Collective Intelligence' of Media Fans" (2002) can be found in H. Jenkins, *Fans, Bloggers, and Gamers* (New York University Press, 2006). I have published other reflections on blogging via *Confessions of an Aca-Fan* (www.henryjenkins.org). See "From YouTube to Youniversity" (Feb. 15, 2007); "Nine Propositions Towards a Cultural Theory of YouTube" (May 27, 2007); "Why Academics Should Blog ... " (April 7, 2008); and "The Message of Twitter: 'Here It Is' and 'Here I Am'" (Aug. 23. 2009). More recently, following the trends, my blog has been complemented with a new podcast (co-hosted with Colin Maclay), *How Do You Like It So Far?* (www.howdoyoulikeitsofar.org).

For examples of alternative models of dialogic and collaborative writing, see my scholarly "Forums on Gender and Fan Culture" (May 31 – Nov. 26, 2007); "Acafandom and Beyond" (June 13 – Sept. 30, 2011); "The State of Fandom Studies" (March 5 – May 12, 2018); "Popular Religion and Participatory Culture" (Sept. 10 – Oct. 15, 2018). See also Nick Couldry and Henry Jenkins, "Participations: Dialogues on the Participatory Promise of Contemporary Culture and Politics," *International Journal of Communication* 8 (2014).

PART I

PARTICIPATORY CULTURE

1

Introduction to Participatory Culture

Early in my blog's history (Nov. 5, 2006), I shared an outtake from a report I wrote for the MacArthur Foundation, *Confronting the Challenges of Participatory Culture*, in which I identified eight defining characteristics of the current media landscape. My goal was to move the discussion of digital media and learning away from an inventory of tools (since the platforms and devices were then, as now, rapidly evolving). Rather, I wanted to discuss larger patterns within the culture that shaped which technologies would be taken up, who could or could not access them, what purposes they might serve, and what status they might hold.

I argued that the contemporary media landscape is:

1 *Innovative*: "New media are created, dispersed, adopted, adapted, and absorbed into the culture at dramatic rates ... Each new technology spawns a range of different uses and inspires a diversity of aesthetic responses as it gets taken up and deployed by different communities of users."

2 *Convergent*: "Every major idea, image, sound, story, brand, and relationship will play itself out across the broadest possible range of media channels.... Convergence is being shaped top-down by the decisions being made by massive media conglomerates who have controlling interests across all possible media systems

and who enjoy the power to insure that their content circu-lates globally.... At the same time, convergence is being shaped bottom-up by the participatory impulses of consumers, who want the ability to control and shape the flow of media in their lives; they want the media they want when they want it and where they want it.... Moreover, these consumers are taking advantage of the new media technologies to respond to, remix and repurpose existing media content; they use the web to talk back to media producers or tell their own stories about fictional characters."

3 *Everyday*: "The technologization of the American home has been an ongoing process across the 20th century.... Media technol-ogies are fully integrated into our everyday social interactions."

4 *Appropriative*: "New technologies make it easy for people to sample and repurpose media images. We can now quote and recontextualize recorded sounds and images (both still and moving) almost as easily as we can quote and recontextualize words. Increasingly, our culture communicates through snippets of borrowed media content.... We want to become a part of the media experiences which matter to us; we want to create and share our own media with others."

5 *Networked*: "Media technologies are interconnected so that messages flow easily from one place to another and from one person to another. Communication occurs at a variety of levels – from intimate and personal to public and large-scale."

6 *Global*: "Media content flows fluidly across national borders; people deploy the new communication networks to interact with others around the world. The global scale of this new media landscape changes the way we think about ourselves and our place in the world."

7 *Generational*: "Recent research suggests that young people and adults live in fundamentally different media environments, using communications technologies in different ways and forming contradictory interpretations of their experiences."

8 *Unequal*: "In so far as participation … represents a new source of power, wealth, and knowledge, it also represents a new site of privilege and inequality…. Expanding access to cyberspace has the potential of empowering new segments of the public to become fuller participants in cultural and civic life, yet we can be concerned by the ability of these electronic technologies to render invisible anyone who is not able to participate."

Taken together, these traits constitute the preconditions for what I call participatory culture. I have defined participatory culture in various ways through the years – for example, describing it as the application of the practices and logics of folk culture to raw materials provided by mass culture (2006), or discussing it in terms of an environment where all are allowed to contribute their own expressive work and receive feedback from those who are more experienced (2009), or analyzing it in terms of a space where multiple voices are heard and are able to have some impact on the decisions that impact their own lives (2016). The first definition speaks to issues of culture; the second, education; and the third, politics and civics. At various points, each of these definitions has been central to my work as I addressed different groups – fans, educators, activists, policy makers. The progression of interviews in this book reflects these different frames for thinking about why participation matters. I am bracketing in this collection a fourth important focus of my work – the ways in which networked culture blurs the lines between consumer and producer, forcing media companies to forge different relationships with their fans. The interviews included in this section speak to broad attributes of participatory culture – in particular, changing conceptions of authorship, creativity, and cosmopolitanism.

I begin the book with the Italian activist/artistic collective, the Wu Ming Foundation, because their story speaks so powerfully to the ways that transformations in the media landscape are resulting in shifts in the status of authors and their relationship with their public. The Wu Ming Foundation, from the start, has refused to accept traditional boundaries between high and low art, between creators and consumers, between individual artists and their collaborators, and between art and politics. My work on participatory culture resonated with them because they were already exploring new forms of performance and storytelling which opened up space for their readers and fans to actively contribute to their creative process, and because they were using their artistic pranks to identify points of vulnerability in the way mass media and professional journalism were currently operating. They were creating works that were designed to be appropriated, that actively encouraged people to take up and extend their artistic projects in new directions. They often did so by masking their own identities so that others would have greater freedom to become the authors of the culture around them. Interestingly, as we are writing, we are seeing the impact of the global appropriation and remixing of their work in the form of the QAnon conspiracy theory. Wu Ming's novel, *Q*, deals with the exploits of a spy for the Roman Catholic church during the sixteenth century, but has been widely read as an allegory for contemporary European politics. *Q* – a transnational best-seller – has been published in 18 languages. The QAnon conspiracy theory refers to a series of revelations from someone who claims to be part of the American deep state and who goes by the name Q. This Q has constructed a narrative that makes Donald Trump the protagonist in a struggle against, among other things, human trafficking, in which Hollywood and the Democratic party are implicated. Here, we see Wu Ming's politics turned upside down, but we also see an extension of some of the tactics by which they had sought to disrupt the communication sector a decade or more earlier.

David Gauntlett and I share a commitment to help promote grassroots creativity, which is central to my conception of participatory culture. But we also share some important disagreements. The one which surfaced during my exchange with him was the difference between his focus on creativity as understood through the frames of folk culture and maker culture, and my own interest in the ways fan communities remix and remake raw materials drawn from mass culture. This disagreement was clearly an important one for both of us: Gauntlett returns to this moment as the focal point for his reflections on the interview. At stake is what it means to create, what relationship exists between artists and the culture around them, how cultural traditions and shared stories might impact their practices, and what forms of acknowledgment they owe to those who come before. Gauntlett's work reminds us that the idea of grassroots creativity has a larger history, that it is visible in the ways folk practices – ranging from stitching and weaving to singing and dancing – were passed down from one generation to the next. He is interested in exploring what value people placed on the things they made with their own hands, as opposed to the readymade objects of industrial culture. And he is interested in the ways the digital is enabling new platforms for people to share what they make with each other.

My conversation with Ethan Zuckerman asks whether our use of networked communications technology really fulfills the potentials many of us saw for a more global circulation of ideas. Zuckerman is almost certainly the most cosmopolitan person I know – always a bit jet-lagged because of his brutal travel schedule, connected through his work on Global Voices with bloggers who write knowingly about social and political movements in their countries, helping to develop new tools and practices for connecting people together through his work at the MIT Media Lab's Center for Civic Media. This interview was shaped by the context of the Arab Spring movement which he was tracking closely. Many in the west had been excited by the ways in which Twitter allowed the perspectives of those resisting – and in some cases overturning – longstanding and repressive governments in the Middle East to be communicated quickly and directly with supporters around the world. Yet, these exchanges resulted in misunderstandings and raised false expectations because they were not grounded in the kinds of ongoing exchanges that might allow us to better understand each other. What he calls "incomplete globalization" reflects the difference between spectacular examples of "global" communication and the "everyday" aspects of participation in a networked culture.

Further Reading

My ideas about participatory culture have been central to my writing through the years. You can see these concepts take shape through: *Textual Poachers: Television Fans and Participatory Culture* (New York: Routledge, Chapman and Hall, 1992); *Convergence Culture: Where Old and New Media Collide* (New York University Press, August 2006); *Fans, Bloggers, and Gamers: Exploring Participatory Culture* (New York University Press, August 2006); Henry Jenkins with Ravi Purushotma, Margaret Weigel, Katie Clinton, and Alice J. Robison, *Confronting the Challenges of Participatory Culture: Media Education for the 21st Century* (Cambridge, MA: MIT Press, 2009); Henry Jenkins and Wyn Kelley, with Katie Clinton, Jenna McWilliams, Ricardo Pitts-Wiley, and Erin Reilly, *Reading in a Participatory Culture: Remixing Moby-Dick for the English Literature Classroom* (New York: Teacher's College Press, 2013); Henry Jenkins, Sam Ford, and Joshua Green, *Spreadable Media: Creating Meaning and Value in a Networked Culture* (New York University Press, January 2013); Henry Jenkins, Mizuko Ito, and danah boyd, *Participatory Culture in a Networked Era* (Cambridge: Polity, 2015); Henry Jenkins, Sangita Shresthova, Liana Gamber-Thompson, Neta Kligler-Vilenchik, and Arely Zimmerman, *By Any Media Necessary: The New Youth Activism* (New York University Press, 2016).

For other perspectives on participatory culture, see my blog interviews with Jean Burgess (Oct. 7, 2007); Axel Bruns (May 9, 2008); Alex Juhasz (Feb. 19, 2009); Paul Booth (Aug. 13, 2010); Howard Rheingold (Aug. 13, 2012); Pat Aufderheide and Ellen Seiter (Oct. 11, 2012); Sarah Banet-Weiser (April 10, 2013); Aaron Delwiche and Jennifer Jacobs Henderson (May 6, 2013); Mirko Tobias Schafer (May 12, 2013); Daren Brabham (Oct. 2, 2013); Limor Shiffman (Feb. 17, 2014); John Banks (May 9, 2014); Aran Seinnreich (Oct. 29, 2014); Stuart Cunningham and David Craig (April 21, 2016); Ann M. Pendleton-Jullian (Nov. 17, 2016); Adam Fish (April 27, 2017); Whitney Phillips and Ryan M. Milner (May 30, 2017). I have also run two series which look at participatory culture in specific cultural contexts – Poland (Nov. 22 – Dec. 6, 2013) and the Czech Republic (Feb. 21 – March 1, 2018).

For more on the Wu Ming Foundation and QAnon, see *How Do You Like It So Far?* (Episode 22).

2

How *Slapshot* Inspired a Cultural Revolution: The Wu Ming Foundation (2006)

Wu Ming is a band of writers that formed in January 2000 after the end of the multi-use collective moniker experience known as the Luther Blissett Project. Wu Ming wrote several novels, including *Q* (1999), *54* (2002), *Manituana* (2007), *Altai* (2009), *The Army of Sleepwalkers* (2014), and *Proletkult* (2018), as well as hard-to-categorize nonfiction books, the most recent of which is *Un Viaggio Che Non Promettiamo Breve* [*No Promise That This Trip Will Be Short*] (2018), a narrative history of No Tav, the mass movement effectively opposing – since 1991 – the construction of a high-speed railroad between Italy and France.

You talked about the Luther Blissett movement as "grassroots mythmaking," comparing it with fan fiction and contrasting it with the culture jamming movement. What do you see as the value of grassroots mythmaking?

Wu Ming (WM) 1: While there's a tendency to use "myths" as a fancy synonym of "lies," I'd like to stick to a more precise definition. To put it very simply, myths are stories that keep communities alive and together. We couldn't interact with each other without the bonds we create by swapping stories, and myths are stories with the strongest symbolic value, stories that hint at the mysteries of how we all came to be here, how we're managing to get along in some way, and what the future looks like.

Myths are not weird stuff from an ancient past, they keep changing shape and context, and they always belong to the present day, they tell us about us here and now. Even the most rational of people recognize the power of myths in their life. As Joseph Campbell once pointed out, if you look at any professor at play in a bowling alley, and "watch him twist and turn after the ball has left his hand, to bring it over to the standing pins," you'll see that he's trying to summon supernatural powers, the same we find in myths and folk tales populated by demons, witches, magicians, gods, etc.

Moreover, myths have a very important function: they can incite abused people into fighting back, as stories of injustice and rebellion, repression and resistance, are handed down from one generation to the next. For example, Martin Luther King and Malcolm X are both historical and mythical figures, they're the beloved martyrs, the guys who dared to stand up and tell the truth and paid dearly for this. On the other hand, myths persuade suffering people to endure their situation and hope for a settling of scores, as in the myth of the Final Judgment, when the last shall be first, or the myth of revolution, when the poor shall take over and eat the rich.

In the early/mid 1990s, the "Luther Blissett" collective identity was created and adopted by an informal network of people (artists, hackers, and activists) interested in using the power of myths, and moving beyond agit-prop "counter-information." In Bologna, my circle of friends shared an obsession with the eternal return of such archetypal figures as folk heroes and tricksters. We spent our days exploring pop culture, studying the language of the Mexican Zapatistas, collecting stories of media hoaxes and communication guerrilla warfare since the 1920s (Berlin Dada stuff, futuristic soirées, etc.), obsessively re-watching one particular movie, *Slapshot* by George Roy Hill, starring Paul Newman as hockey player Reggie Dunlop. We liked Reggie Dunlop very much – he was the perfect trickster, the Anansi of African legends, the Coyote of Native American legends, Ulysses manipulating the cyclops' mind. What if we could build our own "Reggie Dunlop," a "trickster with a thousand faces," a golem made of the clay of three rivers – the agit-prop tradition, folk mythology, and pop culture? What if we started a completely new role-play game, using all the media platforms available at the time to spread the legend of a new folk hero, a hero fueled-up by collective intelligence? ...

We were in touch with many people in Italy and abroad – thanks to BBS (bulletin board system) networks like FidoNet, the mail art network, and the national scene of occupied social centers. We spread the word and it all happened very quickly. In a few months, hundreds of people were using the "Luther Blissett" name and the new golem was getting a lot of coverage by baffled journalists. Yes, there was a disruptive element, a confrontational stance, something that made us cousins of "culture jammers," "subvertisers," or theorists like the Critical Art Ensemble, etc., but there was an important difference. Adbusters-type disturbance was all right, screwing up corporate propaganda is probably a necessary phase to go through: make parodies of advertisements, criticize consumerism, those are certainly good deeds ... However, Luther Blissett also had a more positive attitude – the main purpose was to create a community around Blissett's myth. Pranks, media stunts, and culture jamming were more the means to spread the myth than the ends of the project. The most important aspect of our activities was not sabotage, but the way sabotage increased Blissett's mythical status.

It was an amazing upheaval, so many people writing, acting, performing under the same pseudonym, coordinating their efforts in some way without the need to know each other, by sending each other messages in bottles. It was an open, informal community. Fake news and media hoaxes served the purpose of making our very presence on the media landscape legendary, so that ever more people joined us and adopted the name. "Culture jamming" was just a subordinate part of the project: the practical exploration of a grassroots, interactive mythology was the most important thing.

The Wikipedia describes the movement as an "open reputation," implying that the name Luther Blissett was open to being appropriated and used by hundreds of different participants. Can you explain this concept of an "open reputation," and what does it suggest about the nature of authorship in contemporary culture?

WM2: "Open reputation" means that the different participants in the "Multiple Name" game were not shreds of a schizophrenic conflict of personalities: they were all facets of one identity. Every time you used the name "Luther Blissett," you were doing more than adhering to a project: you were becoming Luther Blissett, you were Luther Blissett.

On planet Tlön, the famous fictional world invented by Jorge Luis Borges, "books are rarely signed, nor does the concept of plagiarism exist ... It has been decided that all books are the work of a single author who is timeless and anonymous." It isn't by chance that, according to one of Tlön's philosophical schools, "All men who speak a line of Shakespeare are William Shakespeare."

I think that Luther Blissett was an experiment in practical philosophy. Luther challenged the belief in "the Author as an individual genius" with a moral fable on how creativity really works. We believe that any author is a collective author.

Several years ago, the world of literature was informed that Raymond Carver wasn't really Raymond Carver. Carver's original drafts were much longer than the published versions. All the exceeding parts were cut out by his editor, Gordon Lish. Carver's endings were actually Lish's endings.

I've got a question: what if Mr. Lish weren't an editor, but just a friend of Carver's? Let's imagine that Gordon Lish was a post-office clerk living across the street from Carver. One night, Carver rings Lish's doorbell and says: "Let's go to the bar and have a beer, I need your opinion about the story I'm writing." Carver reads the short story to Lish, and the latter says: "It's good, but it drags on for too long. Why not cut the last paragraph? That would make a sharper ending, wouldn't it?" Carver goes home and follow Lish's advice. We the readers will never know about that conversation. Nothing strange happens. Carver is still Carver, and we're going to talk about Carver's sharp endings, not Lish's.

Now I've got a few more questions: how many authors happen to talk with post-office clerks? How many books are the result of conversations between authors and post-office clerks? How many times does an author get an idea from a person she talks with? And is there something she can do about it? Can she confine herself to an ivory tower in order to save "her own voice?" In that case, except for a diary of her confinement, she'd have nothing to write about.

Storytellers must immerse their hands in the sea of stories, and accept the fact that they are just complexity reducers, "filters" between the mythosphere and the people. There's no "originality" out of this; you can be "original" only in the way you filter and re-elaborate what you get from your community.

As a consequence, stories belong to everyone, and the private property of popular culture is a contradiction in terms. Stories should be free to circulate, fertilize brains, and enhance the open reputation of any author. That's the reason why our books, as physical objects and containers of stories, have a price – so that we make a living out of writing them – while as immaterial stories they can be freely reproduced in an economy that's based upon abundancy instead of scarcity: there can be no maximum amount of stories, the tank can be filled endlessly.

I am tempted to describe the Luther Blissett movement as a fandom without an originating text. How did you go about creating a community around Luther Blissett? How might we compare and contrast what emerged here with a traditional fan community?

WM1: In a way, since every single action done by anybody under the pseudonym ended up expanding and enhancing Luther Blissett's reputation as a hero, we may say that every action was "fan fiction." Fan fiction delves into an originating set of texts (a TV series, a movie and its sequels, etc.) in order to expand the lives of the characters and improve the fan's experience. That's what we did all the time.

In the context of the Luther Blissett Project, we even produced "proper," explicit fan fiction – *Star Trek* fan fiction in particular, e.g. an interview with Capt. Jean-Luc Picard on some architectural absurdities in Bologna. The references to fandom and fan culture were frequent, we were all sci-fi and genre fiction fans (and my brother is an old-time Trekkie).

At the end of 1995, we published a book called *Mind Invaders*, whose first chapter[1] was mainly devoted to discussing the mythopoetical language spoken by Tamarians in a famous episode of *Star Trek: The Next Generation* – you know, phrases like: "Shaka, when the walls fell," or "Sokath, his eyes uncovered." Tamarian language provided us with a way of incorporating tradition into our activities. We often described the LBP (Luther Blissett Project) as a "Picard and Dathon at El Adrel" kind of situation (i.e. working together for a common goal, even without knowing each other). We even broadcasted the whole episode (only the audio, of course) during our local radio show, "Radio Blissett."

Once you've got a situation in which everybody can be the masked hero, it isn't difficult to create a community around this concept. Here's the ensuing virtuous circle: if a whole community takes responsibility for what single members say or do (think of the scene in Stanley Kubrick's *Spartacus* when every captured slave says: "I am Spartacus!"), members will feel themselves surrounded with warmth and complicity, and will be driven to give their best to the project.

Many of the best pranks associated with Luther Blissett seem to have been played upon traditional media – on television producers and print journalists, primarily. How might we see what you did as reflecting the shifting relations between bottom-up grassroots media power and top-down corporate media power?

WM1: In the Italian press, from 1994 to 1999, "Luther Blissett" (whose advent coincided with the rise of the Web) became almost a synonym for "Internet activism" and net-culture. Traditional journalists felt both fascinated and threatened by this "new media" thing – it was growing so fast and they were totally unprepared, unable to understand. They couldn't find words for such a complex social trend (an epoch-defining shift from top-down communication systems to horizontal networks and personal media!).

They could find words for Luther Blissett though, as the Sheriff of Nottingham could find words for Robin Hood. Luther Blissett was a person – well, sort of, I mean that he was an anthropomorphic figure, he literally embodied what was happening all around. I keep a 10-inch stack of press clippings in my apartment; leaf through it, and you'll find all kinds of definitions for Blissett: "terrorista culturale," "bandito dell'informazione," "pirata informatico," "guerrigliero digitale" ...

In 1996–7, Italy and Europe were swept by a tide of moral panic and mass paranoia on the subject of pedophilia: all of a sudden the Internet was described as an evil place, far more dangerous than any other place, the wood where child abusers lurked behind trees, waiting for Little Red Riding Hood. It didn't matter that in Italy 91 percent of reported child abuses took place in the family and had nothing to do with computers: the Internet was the new folk devil. Traditional gatekeepers had the pretext for venting their anxiety about the Internet, and slandering those who dared to do without them.

That's when the Luther Blissett Project started to pull well-organized media pranks on such morbid subjects as pedophilia, the Internet, and satanic ritual abuse. We wanted to prove that that kind of sensational story was picked up and printed with no fact-checking at all. Some panic-spreaders cut extremely sorry figures because of us. A few of them angrily commented that, by sidetracking the press, we were protecting actual pedophiles. An interesting logic: if there are no pedophiles, we're going to invent them, and if someone proves that we invented them, we'll accuse them of defending pedophiles ... who didn't exist in the first place!

In one particular case, Luther Blissett even conducted a grassroots counter-investigation in a criminal case in Bologna, where a bunch of heavy-metal fans (they called themselves the "Children of Satan") had become scapegoats for the local law authorities. They were arrested during a poorly thought-out operation targeting alleged ritual abusers. No evidence at all, no reliable testimony, nothing. Of course, they were savagely calumniated in the media, at least at the beginning; there was much talk about "secret websites for pedophiles," etc. Luther Blissett, by means of some carefully planned stunts, managed to instill in the public opinion reasonable doubts about the solidity of the case against those guys. In the end, they were fully acquitted and indemnified by the state for 18 months of unjust detention.

Slowly but steadily, moral panic decreased and Luther Blissett switched to other tactics and targets (e.g. the highbrow art world and the Holy See), four of us focused on "Operation Dien Bien Q,"[2] and the whole network prepared for the end of Blissett's Five Year Plan.

As I look back, I understand that Luther Blissett pioneered the collision between old and new media, in a phase when the boundaries of old and new were sharper than they are now, and there were less intersections, only a few newspapers had an online edition, journalists didn't have their own blogs, and file sharing was still far from being a mass phenomenon.

How did the work of the Luther Blissett movement bridge between the online world and physical reality, taking the work of imagination and giving it some real-world consequences?

WM2: Imagination has real-world consequences if it reaches other people's brains. Luther Blissett used mass media as a privileged vehicle for this. On the most trivial level, TV and newspapers replaced Aristotle as the source of "truth" long ago. On the other hand, luckily, many people are capable of critical thinking, and false news can have a greater impact if it is exposed and explained, instead of remaining hidden under the big heap of information.

I'll give two examples: at the beginning of 1994, even before Luther Blissett started his career, some of us coined the slogan "You decide tomorrow's scoop!" and put the concept into practice in the streets. Local newspapers are very penetrable, and their weakest point is the "Letters to the Editor" page. We started to send letters to Bologna's dailies, pretending to be horrified citizens who had found animal entrails on park benches, car windshields, children's swings, and traffic signs. In two weeks, the news moved from letters to feature articles, headlines got bigger and bigger, and journalists found a name for this new phenomenon: "Horrorism." Art critics and sociologists were asked about the meaning of this provocation. Then someone really left a big ox heart hanging from a tree, leaving people bewildered. Emulation was the only real-world consequence ... except for what we learned from the prank, which was a prelude to bigger things.

Two years later, we filled a schoolbag with alleged remnants of a satanic ceremony (black candles, two human shinbones, and a skull), then put it in a luggage locker at the Bologna railroad station. We anonymously sent the deposit receipt to a journalist who was particularly keen on spreading moral panic, along with a communiqué announcing the birth of a new anti-Satanist vigilante group. The story was that "we," the vigilantes, had assaulted Satanists during a black mass, we had beaten them and put them to flight, then we'd stolen that stuff and sent them to the journalist as evidence of our presence in town.

As WM1 said, this was part of our counter-information campaign on the case of the "Children of Satan." However, it was a hot summer, and that particular journalist was on vacation. He went back to work after three weeks, found our letter, paid the fee for a month's storage (about $150), found the skull and the other stuff, and the story made the front page, under a banner headline. He didn't know that we had already claimed responsibility for the prank and explained our motives, on the pages of a local mag. This "preemptive confession" sounded like: "This guy's going to find a schoolbag filled with crap and write a sensational piece about it. After all the lies he spread, at last he reaps as he sowed. We invented one story, but he invented many more."

As a "real-world consequence," everything changed: the guy never wrote about the "Children of Satan" anymore, the other two Bologna daily papers started to question the solidity of the case. It was like a crash course in media education for an entire city. Until that moment, by using the tools of traditional counter-inquiries, we had gotten no results. The "homeopathic" effect of one single lie cured the illness better than the traditional media medicines usually administered to public opinion.

You wrote, "A vast, transnational community of people surrounds us and interacts with our books in a creative way, we encourage all kinds of sharing, reappropriation, derivative works etc." What can you tell me about your relationship to your readers and the forms of appropriative works they produce?

WM2: Since the beginning of our careers as professional storytellers, we have exhorted our readers to get in touch with us and become a sort of collective "sixth member," in constant osmosis with the original group. To be part of the Wu Ming "democratic republic of readers" does not mean having a seat in the front row or a privileged access to our output. It means taking part, in a more or less direct manner, in a process of collective intelligence and creation that we usually compare with the relationship between community and storyteller in old folk culture.

It must be said that this cooperation does not take place only on the Internet; there are also many face-to-face moments, there's warm physical participation, which we deem as absolutely necessary. We're "online" but we're also "on the road."

The Internet allowed us to skip intermediaries such as the publishers' press office and PR department; our presentation tours are completely self-organized. Being a group of five people, Wu Ming is almost ubiquitous, and two or three delegations can discuss our work in different places simultaneously, hundreds of miles apart from each other. We go to places that are usually snubbed by mainstream authors, such as tiny bookshops, public libraries in small villages, squats, sometimes even private apartments – we literally deliver the presentation at home, if there's a group of friends willing to get together one night and listen to what we have to say.

There's constant interaction between us and the readers – they send us comments, suggestions, and criticism. The female characters in our novels have had a positive evolution thanks to the harsh critiques expressed by some female readers. Our newsletter, titled after General Võ Nguyên Giáp, has about 10,000 subscribers and regularly features the readers' feedback: reviews, comments, and pieces on various subjects. We don't rely on any open forum or blog – we tried, but it took too much time to get rid of trolls. We prefer to receive a lot of stuff via email, and make a quality selection.

Having said this, I think that the most explicit invitation to appropriate our work is the "copyleft notice" included in all our books, which can be copied, xeroxed, or downloaded straight from our website. We encourage people to use our works. Our novel *Q* was deconstructed and rewritten as a very original theatrical drama. *54* became the inspiration for an album by folk-rock band Yo Yo Mundi...

WM1: ... not to mention the use of our characters in role-play games. I'll say a few things about this later.

WM2: Even more explicitly, we have launched several collective writing projects. The first one was "I Shall Call You Russell," and it bordered on the commonplace: we wrote the first chapter of a sci-fi novel, and anyone could write and send the following ones. The selection of chapters took place in public, on a temporary blog run by us. A jury selected the three best versions of any chapter, and people could vote for their favorite one, which became the next chapter in the "official" (i.e., collectively approved) sequence, though all the other versions remained available as sources of inspiration, creating a web of plot "bifurcations" and "dead-end streets." There was no "official" last chapter, all the versions were published *ex aequo*.

The most important result of this experiment was the birth of another collective of novelists, Kai Zen (Japanese for "Constant improvement"). Kai Zen themselves have launched more and more projects like that, and their debut novel will be published in a few weeks by the biggest Italian publisher.

The second project was an experiment in "open source literature," as in "open source software." The main difference between storytelling and software programming is that almost everybody can work on the source code of a story. The source code of a story is the story itself. We wrote a short story titled "The Ballad of Corazza" and we put it on line. We asked readers to work on it, be it to change an adjective, rewrite a whole paragraph, or insert a new character. We received alternative versions of the story, did the revisions accordingly, and made the result available.

After a couple of months, we released "The Ballad of Corazza 2.0," which was a consistent synthesis of all suggested modifications. This version was also edited collectively until we had the (potentially) definitive text. The more open nature of this second project managed to stir creativity with greater effectiveness, as "The Ballad of Corazza" has become a graphic novel; a theatrical act (based upon one of the alternative versions); and two different reading performances, one of which had live musical accompaniment, with the score the result of a similar "open source" process.

Last, but absolutely not least, there's the kind of interaction generated by the novels or short stories written by our readers, with no direct connection to our work. Back when we started, we publicly stated that we were willing to read unpublished stuff. Call it "talent scouting" if you like. Well, we received so much stuff (poetry, fiction, scripts, whatever) that we had to wave the white flag. We couldn't possibly read all those novels and short stories, no way.

Our community's collective wisdom solved the problem for us: fifteen *Giap* subscribers responded and volunteered for reading anything submitted by other readers. These people formed a collective on their own, iQuindici (TheFifteen – even if they are about

30 people now). They have their own website[3] and their own e-zine (Inciquid); they organize public readings of the best stuff they receive and select, and promote the adoption of open licenses (creative commons, copyleft, you-name-it) in the Italian publishing industry. Several new authors were "discovered" by publishers thanks to iQuindici ...

What you had was a huge number of people from different backgrounds and geographical areas, all interacting with each other in order to introduce ever-new elements into a legend they were constructing in real time and telling all together. It is important to point out that these people didn't know each other personally, some of them never met, never talked or wrote to each other, not even on the phone, not even via email, for the whole duration of the project. I never met the majority of people who operated under the Luther Blissett pseudonym in other cities, not to mention people calling themselves Luther Blissett in other countries. Right from the beginning, the Bolognese collective (which was more tight-knit than other informal groups springing out all over Italy) labeled itself "the only central committee whose aim is to lose control of the party."

Yes, there was some sort of coordination between the different local groups, and a few things were explicitly prohibited: the Luther Blissett name could not be used to spread racist, sexist or fascist material, and no Luther Blissett material could have a copyright. That's all the "organization" we had.

Most of the time, we ended up taking each other by surprise – we heard the news about a prank pulled by Blissett in Southern Italy and immediately claimed co-responsibility by playing a similar one or by giving a completely different motive for the prank! We enjoyed leaving clues for other Blissetts, and give wild interpretations of the clues left by them. In several cases, the same hoaxes or actions were given different interpretations by different Blissetts "cooperating" with each other. It was all grist to the mill, or, as we say in Italy, "tutto fa brodo" – everything adds to the soup ...

Typically avant-garde work frames itself in opposition to popular culture. Yet it is clear that you are in some senses a fan of popular culture. How would you describe your relationship to the entertainment texts which you draw upon in your work?

WM1: I grew up reading sci-fi pulp books; my room was chock-full of tons of Marvel and DC comics, as well as Italian comics which you've probably never heard of. I spent days watching soccer matches, spaghetti westerns, Bruce Lee movies (or, even worse/better, "Bruce Li" movies and other crap cashing in on Bruce Lee's death), *Star Trek* (every afternoon on a local tv station), British series like *Space 1999*, and funky detective series like *Baretta* and *Starsky & Hutch*. I was a raving fan of Japanese anime, like every other kid I knew. In the late 1970s, *UFO Robot Grendizer*, *Great Mazinger*, and *Steel Jeeg* took Italian television by storm, and episodes were watched by millions of kids. I always listened to all genres of popular music from Italian singer-songwriters to Frank Zappa to LA punk acts like the Germs of Black Flag, through to Tony Bennett and Brazilian Hip Hop. I used to play soccer games on my Commodore 64. I went to the movies as often as I could. I played table games like Monopoly and Scrabble.

In short, I started to expose my brain and body to all kinds of popular culture at a time when the Internet didn't exist. I've always been in love with pop culture. All the other members of Wu Ming have similar backgrounds: sci-fi, comics, martial arts, rock'n'roll – two of them played in punk rock bands, one of which was fairly famous in the Italian underground. I think that, if you don't know pop culture, you don't know your culture, thereby you don't know the world around you. If you don't know shit about pop culture, how can you be on the cutting edge of anything? If you don't soil your hands with pop culture, if you snub and sneer at today's participatory culture, you can't be "avant-garde," no matter how hard you try.

By the way, what does "avant-garde" mean? "Avant-garde" is French for "vanguard," it is a military-connoted term. "Avant-garde" means being at the front point of the battle. Too often, the avant-garde turn around and find out there's no rear-guard, nobody's following them. That's because they marched too fast, or in the wrong direction. This is the common problem of artistic and political vanguards. It didn't happen to Luther Blissett because Luther Blissett was about spreading a disease, plus there was an "educational" aspect. Once a prank had been played successfully, we claimed responsibility and explained it in detail. Explain: that's what the avant-garde never do. Indeed, they enjoy being obscure, they mistake obscure for radical, they don't want to give the people access to their work. They are enemies of the people. We never acted like that: the more people understand what we're doing, the happier we are. From that point of view, we're not exactly "avant-garde."

Reflections

Many things have happened to Wu Ming since the conversation we had with Henry Jenkins in 2006. The interview faithfully portrayed a collective of writers with a lot of fan culture and social cooperation around it, a group collaborating with many other people and taking part in a lot of projects, way beyond their more easily describable activities, like writing novels.

We have always cherished that horizontal aspect of our work. It's thanks to the legacy of Luther Blissett. We had inherited some key characteristics of the project, one of which was the utter refusal of celebrity culture and cultural hierarchies.

At the turn of the decade, the situation evolved at a warp factor of 14.1. We launched a new social-media-innervated blog that inherited the name of our "classic" newsletter, *Giap*. Very soon, it burst with intense, peculiarly long discussions among our readers and fellow travelers: talks about cultural and political subjects, teeming with subthreads and sub-subthreads.

Our community also used the blog's commentary to reflect upon the kind of "creative nonfiction" we had started to write while drifting away from the historical novel form. Books such as *Point Lenana* or the four-volume series *Tetralogy of Paths*. which is still being written. In those books, which we call UNOs (Unidentified Narrative Objects), we tackled many historical, geographical, and environmental issues. We're exploring an intersection between investigative journalism, narrative biography, historical geography, and a postcolonial retelling of Italy's past.

At a certain point, people started to organize into autonomous collectives and "labs," each one of them inspired by our nonfiction. They started their own blogs and established their own social media presence to deal with the issues we had tackled in our UNOs. The fan culture around us became fan activism. That's how the name "Wu Ming Foundation," which we always used half-jokingly, acquired a new, concrete meaning.

Alpinismo Molotov, Nicoletta Bourbaki, and Quinto Tipo are examples of collectives and cultural projects that developed out of our 2010s work. Alpinismo Molotov deals with environmental issues and struggles in Italy's mountainous areas. Nicoletta Bourbaki is a group of historians and researchers debunking right-wing fake news, and countering neo-fascist attempts at manipulating the Italian Wikipedia. Quinto Tipo is a collective of writers and editors experimenting with UNOs. And so on and so forth.

Of course, we also keep writing novels, albeit somewhat different ones from the kind of metahistorical fiction we practiced during the Noughts.

Many writers and artists sincerely respect their fans, but they see themselves like the sun and their fandom as the solar system. It's an obsolete orbital model, which the cultural industry keeps encouraging in spite of all the changes Henry has written about in his books.

We represent ourselves – the Wu Ming collective – as little more than a probability orbit in an electron cloud. Sometimes we have found ourselves near the location of a rather elusive nucleus; other times that place is occupied by other projects. Unfortunately the WMF is still little-known abroad, far less known than our more strictly literary output. However, that's the direction we've taken.

3

Studying Creativity in the Age of Web 2.0: David Gauntlett (2011)

David Gauntlett is Canada Research Chair in Creative Innovation and Leadership in the Faculty of Communication and Design, Ryerson University, Toronto (since 2018). He was previously Professor of Creativity and Design and Director of Research at Westminster School of Media, Arts and Design, University of Westminster, UK. He is the author of several books, including *Creative Explorations* (2007), *Making is Connecting* (2011, second edition 2018), and *Making Media Studies* (2015). He has worked with a number of the world's leading creative organizations, including the BBC, Tate, and LEGO. See website at www.davidgauntlett.com for videos and resources.

Let's start with something very basic – the title of your book, *Making is Connecting*. What do you mean by making? By connecting? What do you see as the relationship between the two in an era of networked computing?

Well, I'm using these words in their recognized senses – I don't believe in making up new words, or jargon, for things that can be expressed simply. So, by 'making', I simply mean people making things. This can be with new technologies or ancient ones, and can be on the Internet or offline. So it refers to James knitting a scarf, Amira writing a poem, Kelly producing a blog, Marvin taking photographs, Michelle making a YouTube video, Jermaine doing a drawing, Natasha coding a videogame, or hundreds of other examples like that.

And 'connecting' means social connections – people starting conversations, sharing reviews, providing information, or making friends. But also it refers, for me, to a connectedness with the world which we live in. So I say 'making is connecting' because you put together ideas and materials to make something new; because creativity often includes a social dimension, connecting you with other people; and because I think that, through making things, you feel more of a participant in the world, and you feel more a part of it, more embedded – because you are contributing, not just consuming, so you're more actively engaged with the world, and, so, more connected.

I think this is almost always the case, regardless of what technology is being used, and was the case for centuries before we had a global wired network. But in an era of networked computing, I think that these benefits are amplified, and many new opportunities and connections are enabled. Creativity didn't begin with the Internet – far from it. But in an obvious and well-known way, the Internet enables people to connect with others who share their interests, regardless of where they live in the world – whereas previously, geography, and the practical difficulties of finding people, made it far more difficult to have conversations with others who shared niche interests.

Having easy access to people who share their passions means that individuals can be inspired by each other's work and ideas – which can lead to a positive spiral of people doing better and better things and inspiring more and more activity by others. This could happen before the Internet, in clubs and societies, but it would tend to be slower, and the inspiring inputs would most likely be fewer, and less diverse.

Across your past couple of books, you have been working through a definition of "creativity." What is your current understanding of this concept and why does understanding creativity seem so urgent at the present moment?

Well I never wanted to get bogged down in arguments over a 'definition' of creativity. But in *Making is Connecting*, I do put forward a new definition, basically to provoke a conversation around how we think about creativity, and to shake up the consensus ... which casually accepts and cites the definition put forward by Mihaly Csikszentmihalyi about 15 years ago. That definition emphasizes that creativity is some kind of novel contribution or innovation which makes a visible difference within a domain of expertise, or in the wider culture. So it's a definition of creativity which requires us to focus on the outputs of a creative process; and then it actually goes further, and says that those outputs don't really count for anything unless they are recognized and embraced by a significant or influential audience.

Now, Csikszentmihalyi developed this definition for a particular purpose – for use in his sociological study of the circumstances which enable creative acts to be recognized and to flourish. So it's fine for his own purposes, and he clearly didn't mean any harm. But now, because Csikszentmihalyi is a well-respected expert in more than one area, widely cited in academic papers and featuring strongly in Google searches in this area, his definition pops up in all kinds of other contexts where someone wants a definition of creativity to put into their talk, article, or presentation.

So the unintended consequence is that creativity is increasingly likely to be understood, these days, as the generation of innovative products which become popular, or at least widely recognized. Now, that is one kind of creativity, but as a definition it seems much too narrow.

One problem is that it runs counter to our common-sense understanding of 'creativity,' because it is far too demanding. I'm sure you can think of quite a few friends or colleagues whom you would say were 'very creative' – and you would really mean it – and yet they have not invented a new process which has revolutionized the field of architecture, and have not written a novel which sold over a million copies, nor done anything else which goes over the very high bar set by Csikszentmihalyi. But you still really believe that these are creative individuals. So that's one difficulty.

Another problem is that this now-standard definition is focused on outputs. Indeed, you can only assess creativity in this way by looking at the outputs of a creative process. I wanted to shift the conversation about creativity so it was more about the process, not the outcomes. But I also thought it was weird that this Csikszentmihalyi perspective on creativity meant that you literally could not say if something was creative or not without consulting an external system of experts or publications. Someone might show you an amazing work of art, or an invention, or a new way to do something, and you might exclaim 'oh that's very creative!', but in strict Csikszentmihalyi terms that would be inaccurate, unless this thing had already become influential or successful.

I talk about all these issues at some length in the book. But I arrive at a definition which emphasizes the process of creativity, rather than outcomes, and prioritizes feelings rather than levels of external success. It's a bit long. It says:

Everyday creativity refers to a process which brings together at least one active human mind, and the material or digital world, in the activity of making something. The activity has not been done in this way by this person (or these people) before. The process may arouse various emotions, such as excitement and frustration, but most especially a feeling of joy. When witnessing and appreciating the output, people may sense the presence of the maker, and recognize those feelings.

I also did a shorter one, trying to make it a single sentence: 'Everyday creativity refers to a process which brings together at least one active human mind, and the material or digital world, in the activity of making something which is novel in that context, and is a process which evokes a feeling of joy.'

This shorter definition is OK, although for the sake of brevity it misses out some bits that I thought were quite important. But, in both cases, you can see I have emphasized emotion – even the word 'joy', which comes through strongly in interviews with makers. They are not filled with joy all the time, of course – creative work is often experienced as hard and challenging – but you get moments of pride and accomplishment which make it all worthwhile.

Understanding creativity is perhaps no more or less important today than at any other time. But we do see, I think, an explosion of visible, accessible, shareable creativity online, which it is interesting and important to study and understand, and which is so diverse, and done by people just because they want to, that I wanted us to have a working definition of creativity which embraced the key dimensions of this work – rather than sniffily dismissing it because it had not yet won awards, gone global, or made an auditable impact.

In particular, I was very taken by your claim that "creativity is something that is felt, rather than something that needs external expert verification." Can you spell out a little more the internal and external dimensions of everyday creativity? On what basis, from what perspective, can it be appraised?

Well, as you can tell, I'm not so bothered about an understanding of creativity which can be counted or quantified. So it's a bit like 'happiness'. On the one hand, as economists and social scientists have found quite recently, happiness is perfectly measurable – you can do large-scale surveys which ask people to say how happy they are with their lives, on a scale of one to five, for instance, and then you can compare with other data and variables, and build up a picture of the self-reported levels of happiness in different groups or areas, and the factors which are correlated with them. Those statistics are really interesting – and indeed I use some of them in *Making is Connecting* to show the importance of personal relationships and creative projects. But, of course, this data doesn't tell you anything about what happiness feels like.

I think creativity is in the same boat. The most important thing about it is what it does for the person doing the creating – the sense of self-esteem, the sense of doing something in the world, being an active participant, feeling alive in the world – these are all feelings which are reported by people who make things in the physical world and, with striking similarity, by people who make things online. But the things they make are also important – those are the things which, at first, connect us with others, which say something about ourselves, and which perhaps contain ideas or inspiration which will make a significant difference to our own or other people's future experiences of the world. So the internal and external dimensions of creativity are both important, but I would say that the most important thing is just doing it.

You suggest early on that the key question you want to answer is "Why is everyday creativity important?" I'll bite: why is everyday creativity important?

I think there is a tendency to think of everyday people's acts of creativity as 'nice', on an individual level, but insignificant, in social or political terms. So it may be personally pleasing, or emotionally rewarding, for someone to make a toy for their child, or to maintain a blog about their everyday experiences, or to make some amusing YouTube videos, or to record and share a song – these all sound like 'nice' things, and nobody would really want to stop them from happening – but they are not considered to be much more than that.

And as you know yourself, Henry, there are people who work on the more obvious, formal 'political' issues in media and communications studies – government broadcasting policies, or the business practices of multinational corporations, or the impact of political advertising on public opinion – and they would not recognize an interest in everyday creativity as part of serious or proper critical study.

But I think these acts of everyday creativity are extremely important. You can cast them as just 'a nice thing' for individuals – and normally they are a nice thing for individuals – but they are much more than that. Every time someone decides to make something themselves, rather than buying or consuming something already made by someone else, they are making a distinct choice, to be an active participant in the world rather than an observer or a shopper in the world. And through the process of making, they get to enjoy, as I've said, that sense of purpose and connection, and satisfaction.

Taken one by one, these are all small things, seemingly insignificant moments; but when more and more people make more and more choices like this, and then also when they go online to amplify and inspire further activities, it builds up to something really big, and powerful.

One of the real revelations in the book for many readers will be how directly the ideas of John Ruskin and William Morris speak to contemporary issues in the Web 2.0 era. What do you see as the key value of re-examining their work now? What do you see as the most important continuities and discontinuities between their conception of craft and contemporary DIY culture?

I'm glad you liked that part. Thank you. I just thought it was very striking that these English Victorian critics, whose philosophy inspired the Arts and Crafts movement, who were writing 120–160 years ago, seemed to really chime with the spirit of Web 2.0, or at least the best part of it. By which I mean: fostering and encouraging everyday creativity, and giving people tools which enable them to share, communicate, and connect. And seeing the importance of things being made by everyday, non-professional people – and the power of making, in itself – rather than us all being mere consumers of stuff made by other people. That's what Ruskin and Morris's most exciting writings are all about.

And, of course, I like making these connections between things that at first look very different. What, for instance, could medieval cathedrals have to teach us about the ecology of YouTube? Well: John Ruskin was passionate about the gargoyles that you find on medieval cathedrals. They are often quite quirky and ugly, and rather roughly done – not at all like 'fine art' – but that's precisely why Ruskin cherishes them: because you can see in them the lively spirit of a creative human being. And you can sense the presence of the person who spent time making it.

Then, if you carry that way of seeing over to YouTube: there again, you have quite a lot of quirky things, often roughly done, and not like the kind of professional stuff you would see on TV; but that is what makes them so special, and exciting, because what you see there is people making things, and sharing them with others, just because they want to. They've got something they want to communicate. You can often sense that personal presence, and enthusiasm. So Ruskin's passion for one kind of craft really helped me to build an argument about the importance of another.

Then, if you look at what William Morris did with Ruskin's ideas – Morris was more concerned with societies and communities than Ruskin was, and he added a vision of communities connected through the things that they make: people filling their lives with the fruits of their own creative labour. It was especially important to him that people should be creators, not (only) consumers.

Morris felt you had to make things to understand them fully, which is part of the *Make* magazine positive-hacker ethos that is enjoying a revival today. Morris was a maker himself, and mastered a dazzling number of craft and construction techniques. So he was both a writer and a maker, but these were not two separate tracks in his life; rather, his writings and the things he made can be seen as two sides of the same project: 'visionary accounts of an ideal world'.

In ways that seem very relevant today, Morris argued that the route to pleasure and fulfilment was through the collection and dissemination of knowledge, communication between people, and creating and sharing expressive material. That's like a manifesto for Web 2.0, right there. So I think the continuities between these old arguments and our present situation are strong; and the discontinuities are the things that put us in a stronger position today, because today we have much wider access to tools to make and share things, which were denied to non-elite people in the past. Not everyone, of course, has access or the necessary skills, and the tools are often owned by big powerful companies, as we will discuss below – it's not perfect.

But I hope these ideas from Ruskin and Morris are therefore shown not to be just some kind of nostalgia that only shines a little light upon our present situation; rather, they offer very relevant manifestos for what we should be doing today....

In talking about *Star Wars Uncut*, you touch on an issue very important to my own work – can we create using borrowed materials? Does it matter if those raw materials are physical objects (recycling of trash or driftwood, say, as the basis of new artworks, or fabric scraps as the basis for quilting) or media content (as in many forms of fan productivity)? How would you situate fan culture within the larger logic of DIY Media?

Ah, this is interesting – this is where I think my priorities might be a bit different from yours, Henry, perhaps. Of course, there's lots of lovely, amazing stuff out there made by fans. I talk about *Star Wars Uncut* in the book as one of the things that led me to reflect that the kind of tangible joyfulness involved in the process of creativity, which you can get a sense of in its outputs, is more important than the empirical originality of the outputs. *Star Wars Uncut* is a project by fans to remake *Star Wars* in 15-second chunks. There's a huge amount of inventiveness on display in the many different kinds of animation and re-creation which fans have used to produce this amazing patchwork, and it's the funny little homemade details that make it especially touching.

But the thing that I don't like about the emphasis on 'fans' as the new generation of creators is that they are inevitably positioned as, to some extent, subservient to the producers of the big, mainstream (or at least industrial or professional) media thing or things that they are fans of.

So, on the one hand, the fans do very clever, very creative things within their fan practice. But, at the same time, they are not the 'ultimate' creators, but instead take their inspiration from the successful professional media producers who are, in this sense, the 'ultimate' creators. So it seems a bit of an odd emphasis to me. There's so much wholly original stuff out there in the DIY/online creative world, and I think the focus on 'fans' may tend to feed the egos of professional media producers who feel they are the rightful creators of original content – the kind of authentic creative work that ordinary mortals could not make and which such mortals could, at best, only be 'fans' of. Do you know what I mean? As advocates of a new, alternative participatory culture, I don't think we should always pick examples that are derivatives of, or in some way dependent upon, the offerings of the traditional established media.

We may have to agree to disagree on some of this. Yes, fans are not the only form of participatory culture out there and part of what I love about this book is that you really engage with a broader array of DIY practices. For me, participatory culture would refer to any form of cultural practice which is open to a broad range of participants who have access to the means of cultural production and circulation. My own work has focused primarily on fans because this is a form of cultural production I have been tracing – and engaging with – for more than 30 years, but, in my forthcoming book *Spreadable Media,* we deal with a much wider array of participatory-culture communities. Sites like YouTube and Flickr and Etsy have certainly increased the visibility of these other sites of grassroots production. Fans interest me because they inhabit the intersection between the old media culture and the new, and thus they illustrate the contradictions of a moment of media in transition. But I am not saying that they are more creative than any of a range of other communities who are similarly transitioning from the pre-digital to the digital.

That said, I do not see fans as "subservient" to commercial media, any more than I see any artist as "subservient" to the raw materials out of which they construct their art. So, let's imagine a range of different DIY makers. One of them works within a genre

and builds on its established icons and their encrusted media. One reconstructs historical artifacts and thus builds on the crafts of the past. One works within a tradition and thus starts from a set of practices inherited from other crafters. One remixes existing media content and thus builds upon the meanings and associations contained there. One takes discarded Coke bottles as physical material out of which they construct something new. For me, there is nothing fundamentally different about these processes. All are working with the resources they draw from the culture around them to create something new and distinctly theirs.

I am purposefully avoiding assigning high or low cultural status to these practices because any of the above could end up in a gallery space or a craft fair or fan convention in the current context, and any could be posted online. Cultural hierarchies work to make fan production "less valuable" than, say, the work of a postmodern artist dealing with the same materials, or "less authentic" than a traditional craftsman doing, say, "primitive" art about biblical characters.

As critics, we may be interested in these objects from many different vantage points. A media scholar might be interested in what the fan work says about the program to which it responds, but I might also be interested in the relations *between* the fans and leave the commercial producer out of the equation altogether. I might, for example, study how different DIY communities pass along craft and knowledge from more experienced to newbie participants, and, in that study, the sources of the raw materials are going to be less important to my analysis than the sources of the knowledge being exchanged between participants. But, in terms of whether the participants are being "creative" or not, these differences in source materials are not that important to me.

Yes, you're right, of course – everything builds on some things that have come before, whether it is ways of using materials, or styles and genres of creative work, or the elements and practices of storytelling. I certainly did not mean to suggest that fans who make stuff within an already-existing narrative are 'less creative' than other makers. It was just that it means that the grand narratives, or the powers to create original story universes, remain in the hands of traditional media. But no matter. As you say, creative fans are just as interesting as creative anybody, and working at the 'intersection' between old and new media can be especially revealing.

I was struck by the passage you quote from Ivan Illich:

> **A good educational system should have three purposes: it should provide all who want to learn with access to available resources at any time in their lives; empower all who want to share what they know to find those who want to learn it from them; and finally, furnish all who want to present an issue to the public with the opportunity to make their challenges known.**

It struck me that you could swap out "educational system" with "communication system" and come up with a pretty good definition of what I and others call participatory culture. By these criteria, how would we evaluate the current state of web culture?

I agree, it's a good aspirational definition of participatory culture, or for the Web in general. We are not there yet, but the potential is still there. Some commentators write as though the Web has already been entirely taken over by the big commercial companies, such as Google, or that Web 2.0 has been entirely absorbed by them as a profit machine. I would really hate for that to happen. But to act like it has already happened is, in a way, giving up, I think; and reveals a lack of awareness of what's really going on.

Yes – you offer some sharp criticisms in the book of some contemporary critical studies work which has seen Web 2.0 largely, if not exclusively, as a form of exploitation. How would you situate your work in regard to current debates about "free labor" in the digital economy?

48

Well, basically, I argue that those people who are only interested in saying that Web 2.0 is about the exploitation of free labour are making a category error, and using an exclusively economic lens when that actually isn't the best way of understanding what's happening. Someone who makes an original music video, say, to share with their friends, and with anyone else who wants to take a look, and who chooses to do so by putting it on YouTube, a convenient and free platform, is hardly being 'exploited' in the way we would normally use the term in a Marxist analysis of labour. Obviously, those services do seek to make profit from the advertising revenue, and from the value of the user data that they capture, on the back of stuff provided for free by users. But users themselves see it as a decent bargain – the site hosts your material for free, and enables you to engage with a community around it, and in return it gets to keep that associated revenue. In most cases, the value associated with any particular video or other piece of content will be very small, and it is only when it is multiplied by millions of other bits of content that it becomes a viable business.

These arguments create confusion about what Web 2.0 is about. A really great, archetypal example of Web 2.0 in action would be if there were an encyclopaedia which was entirely written by users around the world, writing about the things that interest and engage them, and collaboratively editing it to make it get better and better. And it would be owned and run by a nonprofit foundation. What an outrageous and unlikely idea! But that already happens, of course, and it's called Wikipedia.

Another archetypal example of Web 2.0 in action would be if an international consortium of organizations – such as, say, a collaboration between the Library of Congress, and the British Library, and perhaps the BBC, and some of the great European museums or cultural institutions – were to set up and support, but not interfere with, a non-commercial platform for creativity, along the lines of YouTube, where people could share their creative works, comment and rate the work of others, and form supportive groups and communities of practice. That one hasn't happened yet, but there's no reason why it couldn't.

Web 2.0, or participatory culture, is not inherently commercial, and it might be healthier and more reliable in a non-commercial environment. One of the best things about non-commercial Web 2.0 services is that they make those comments about 'exploitation of labour' immediately redundant. The critics of the commercial services are not entirely wrong, but they are missing the most important thing that's going on.

Reflections

This interview was conducted in the summer of 2011, when my book *Making is Connecting* had just come out. (There's now a revised and expanded second edition, 2018.) I was very pleased to be invited to have a conversation about it with Henry Jenkins. He was a generous interviewer, praising aspects of my work that differed from his own, and steering the discussion into fruitful areas where I would have something to say.

I was glad to talk about my book, but also I was interested to discuss with Henry the thing that I had always found curious about his work – the focus on 'fans'. I felt that the emphasis on people who were primarily fans of other people's stuff – professional mainstream media stuff – was odd, assigning value to big mainstream media just as new technologies were giving us the opportunity to escape commercial one-size-fits-all media altogether.

Henry's response – see above – is robust, although personally I like it if people are creating their *own* worlds to play in, rather than borrowing one established by a media corporation. But, ultimately, as Henry points out, it's what people *do* with it that counts.

Since we conducted this interview, it has become significantly more apparent that all the positives of online creativity and sharing have been accompanied by a whole pile of negatives. From the mass surveillance machines that present themselves as social media platforms, to the suffocating cultures of online harassment and abuse – the human sources of which we can't even blame on technology companies, though Lanier (2018) has made the case that social media business models are built to amplify our worst tendencies – we see a regrettable slew of awful developments. For those of us who want to be optimistic, and to find solutions – how can we respond?

First, we have to observe that pretty much all of the positive things that we ever said about Internet culture remain true today – all the potential is still there. But all the bad developments exist too. There's a pile of really good things, a pile of really bad things, and neither pile extinguishes the other or makes those things unimportant. But we still need to address this situation.

So I think we have to double down on emphasizing the values of creativity, inclusion, kindness, and inspiration. What else can we do? We can't just give up. And so we have to affirm that creativity, freely expressed and shared, for no reason other than *because we want to*, is powerful and exciting and makes a real difference. We then need platforms for creativity – online, offline, and both – which support creative sharing and the exchange of inspiring ideas, and facilitate supportive and thoughtful feedback. (Some principles for such 'platforms for creativity' are proposed in Gauntlett, 2018.)

We also need to be aware that each online space is more friendly and inviting to members of some groups than of others, and that even the worthwhile 'maker movement' comes with a set of aesthetics and assumptions which are attractive to some people, but off-putting to others. The hype about connected communities and makerspaces doesn't really work if you feel intimidated or bewildered or just plain not-recognized by those environments. So we need to work to transform that too.

The dream of an open creative culture has not changed. The path to get there remains messy and colourful and not at all straightforward, but at least there's some interesting work to do.

References

Gauntlett, D. (2018). *Making is Connecting: The Social Power of Creativity, from Craft and Knitting to Digital Everything.* 2nd expanded edn. Cambridge: Polity.

Lanier, J. (2018). *Ten Arguments for Deleting All Your Social Media Accounts Right Now.* New York: Henry Holt.

4

Digital Cosmopolitans: Ethan Zuckerman (2014)

Ethan Zuckerman is Director of the Center for Civic Media at MIT, and Associate Professor of the Practice of Media Arts and Sciences at the MIT Media Lab and Comparative Media Studies at MIT. He is co-founder of the online community Global Voices, which works to build international understanding through citizen media. His forthcoming book on civics and mistrust will be published by W. W. Norton in 2019.

Much of the media discussion around the Arab Spring movements has centered on the fantasy of more person-to-person communications across borders via social media, rather than through the more formal relations between nations or the mediated communications of traditional journalism. Why has this fantasy of a "Twitter Revolution" proven so compelling to people when their everyday practices often involve relatively limited communications outside of their immediate circles of friends and families?

Like many compelling fantasies, the Twitter Revolution myth has some roots in fact. Tunisia's revolution had a strong media component. Protests in Sidi Bouzid would likely have been invisible to the rest of Tunisia and the rest of the world had they not been documented on Facebook, edited and contextualized by Nawaat.org, and amplified by

Al Jazeera. And there are deep ties between activists in Tunisia and in Egypt that helped spread the ideology and tactics of those revolutions via social media. But any account of the Arab Spring that doesn't focus on existing labor movements, soccer fan-clubs, neighborhood organizations, and other forms of offline social organizing misses the point.

I think Twitter Revolutions are such a compelling idea because they allow us to inscribe ourselves on global events. If digital media are the key actor in a political event, and we're participating by amplifying tweets online, we are part of the revolution, an exciting and compelling prospect. And there are times when this, too, is true – if an event is visible locally and invisible globally, and we take responsibility for translating and amplifying it, leading to global coverage, we might, in fact, share some credit for changing circumstances on the ground.

But this ability to be a participant in a minor way in a global event tends to blind us to our more ordinary use of these media. Very few of us are Andy Carvin, using our online presence to curate digital media and connect our readers to global events. Our use of these tools tends to be about connecting with friends and interests that are far closer to home. There's nothing inherently wrong with that – it's fine for social media to be a tool that connects us locally if we have other media that inform and connect us globally. What strikes me as dangerous is the illusion of connection – the compelling idea that we are encountering global perspectives via digital media when we're mostly reinforcing local ones.

You write, "[New Media] tools help us to discover what we want to know, but they're not very powerful in helping us discover what we might need to know." This seems to be a central theme of your book (*Digital Cosmopolitans: Why We Think the Internet Connects Us, Why It Doesn't and How to Rewrite It* [2014]): that we have opened up new channels of communication which might allow us to connect with others around the world, but that our use of those tools has been limited by a lack of motivation or understanding. We seek out information only about those topics we already care

about, and a large part of the world falls outside of that zone of interests. What are some of the signs that our interest in the world is more limited than our technological reach at the present time?

I think the main reminder is the sense of surprise that pervades much of modern life. The Arab Spring was a surprise, but only up to a point. For those few watching Tunisian social media, it became clear pretty quickly that something deeply unusual and transformative was taking place. At Global Voices, we were able to see the protests unfolding weeks before they received attention in mainstream American media. There's a strong tendency in our contemporary media environment to pay attention to stories only when they've reached a crisis point – we're always arriving in the fourth act, and we never stay through the denouement. It's possible to imagine a form of media that's scanning the horizons and giving us a better sense of what's coming, not what's already arrived.

I think a second reminder is our ability to turn on global networks at moments of crisis. The global response to SARS was quite amazing – within a week of identifying a new syndrome, the WHO had global video-conferences that allowed frontline medical personnel to identify symptoms and jointly diagnose new cases. Once those networks were set up, the spread of the disease slowed dramatically. When we need international connection, we're capable of bringing it about very quickly.

One of the reasons the book has been challenging to describe is that this question you're asking – what are we missing when we're so tightly attached to local media? – is a really hard one to answer. I tend to understand it in personal terms. I follow African media, particularly West African media, quite closely, due to my long personal ties to the region, and, as a result, I see stories well in advance of their visibility in broader media. And while that sounds self-congratulatory, patting myself on the back for my global vision, the actual experience is more anxiety-producing, because it's a perpetual reminder of how much there is to know and discover. The little I know about Nigerian politics that most Americans don't is a perpetual reminder of how much else is going on in the world, and how little we encounter until it manifests as a crisis or emergency.

What roles do the news media play in shaping what we care about, and, conversely, to what degree does our lack of concern or interest impact what the news media are prepared to cover?

I think this relationship between caring and coverage matters much more than it did a generation ago. Newspapers include stories on a wide range of topics – local, national, and international. Until recently, our sense for what readers wanted to hear about came from news-stand sales and letters to the editor, very inexact tools for understanding which stories were being read and which were being ignored. Now we have incredibly granular information, that shows interest on a story-by-story level, including readership and time spent per reader per article. Publishers are acutely aware of these statistics, and more editors and writers are becoming aware of these figures. It becomes harder and harder for authors to report on stories that don't already have an audience, as there's a very strong temptation to write what people want to hear, as they will reward you with their attention.

This becomes a circular equation, because people need help developing an interest in new topics. A fascinating story isn't immediately apparent or comprehensible to an audience. Take the mortgage crisis a few years back – most coverage focused on the moment-to-moment details, featuring stories that were comprehensible to financial professionals and few others. *This American Life* made a major investment – an hour-long story called "The Giant Pool of Money" – that helped audiences understand the crisis and become better consumers of future stories on the situation. If we wanted people to pay attention to protests in Sudan (people beyond those of us who are already watching those protests), we'd need to invest time, energy, and reader attention in explaining the context and importance ... and we'd be gambling that we were able to create an audience for that story in the future.

The net result of this cycle, I fear, is that we get an enormous amount of information on stories we "know" are important – the minutiae of US federal elections and the machinations of Congress – and very little information on parts of the world we know little about, care little about, and care little about because we hear little about them.

I've often thought that there might be a need to shift from a focus on international news (news about things happening elsewhere on the planet) to global news (news that shows the connections between distant events and people in our own communities). Would such an approach help resolve the gaps you are describing here? Why or why not?

I think we'd gain a great deal from journalism that helped to contextualize global events in local terms. The best newspapers and broadcasters have historically tried to do this – one of the losses we experience when local newspapers cut international bureaus is the connection between global stories and local communities.

We need something broader, I suspect, as not every event in Myanmar has an immediate local connection. Sometimes we need heroes and heroines – think of Malala in Pakistan and the ways in which her story has been a window into gender and educational issues in that part of the world. While we can go too far and turn a story about issues into a story about a single person, we often benefit from stories that let us feel like we know and care about an individual in another country or culture.

I think we also need to learn how to tell stories that look at local facets of global issues. A story such as climate change is critically important, but extremely difficult to report. We might benefit from an approach to reporting that showed us the implications for different people in different communities, interweaving personal stories with the science and politics of the issues.

The word "cosmopolitanism" is often used and often misunderstood. What does the term mean to you? What do you see as the core values or virtues of adopting a more cosmopolitan perspective?

I debated whether or not to use the word "cosmopolitanism" in the book, as it evokes a sense of globe-hopping placelessness that's not what I wanted to evoke. But I ended up using it because I found Kwame Appiah's thinking about cosmopolitanism so helpful. Appiah, a Ghanaian-American philosopher, suggests that cosmopolitans recognize that there is more than one acceptable way to live in the world, and that we may have obligations to people who live in very different ways than we do. This, he argues, is one of the possible responses to a world where we find ourselves interacting with people from very different backgrounds. Cosmopolitanism doesn't demand that we accept all ways of living in the world as equally admirable – he works hard to draw a line between cosmopolitanism and moral relativism – but does demand that we steer away from a fundamentalist or nationalist response that sees our way as the only way, and those who believe something different as inferior or unworthy of our consideration or aid.

I'm struck by how personal a response Appiah's cosmopolitanism is. He navigates two very different cultures in his life – his academic life in Princeton and his family in Ghana – and aspects of that life, notably his homosexuality, can be very controversial in one environment and uncontroversial in another. The solution he proposes, it struck me, is one of the more thoughtful approaches to life in a world where we continually encounter other ways of thinking and living.

A cosmopolitan approach offers us the encouragement to discover other ways of solving a problem, while accepting the idea that we may choose to continue living in ways we have in the past. What we are not free to do is to dismiss other ways of living out of hand, or to fall back on a narrow, tribal definition of obligation. It strikes me as a responsible reaction to a world that is connected in ways large and small, in ways we rarely see or understand.

You discuss across the book the symptoms of an "incomplete globalization." Is it incomplete in the sense that it is broken, or incomplete in the sense that it is still in process?

One of the criticisms I've received about the book is that it's insufficiently critical of contemporary global capitalism. One reason critics have brought up that objection is that I'm enthusiastically pro-globalization, though not in the ways most people use that term. I've been involved with global economic development for the past two decades, and it has persuaded me that what developing economies need is more globalization, not less. Nations that have the hardest time educating their populations and giving them economic opportunities tend to be those most detached from global trade and migration flows. This doesn't mean that I support exploitative globalization, and I think that a great deal of what happens at the WTO and other international trade fora is rigged against developing nations. But the enemy isn't globalization – it's bad, unfair globalization.

I use "incomplete globalization" as a way of describing a tension between three types of movement. Atoms are quite free to move across global borders – we've built trade systems that allow low-cost sourcing of raw materials and manufactured goods from across continents and oceans. While trade in atoms isn't barrier free, it's far less restrained than the flow of people, which has been dramatically restrained in the twentieth century, to the great detriment of many in the developing world. I am deeply influenced by Lant Pritchett's arguments, which make the case that increased migration would be the single biggest step taken towards economic development in poor nations. My contribution to the debate is to note that globalization of bits often lags behind globalization of atoms, closely following the globalization of people. I am concerned that a world where we globalize atoms and not bits is a dangerous world – we are dependent on other parts of the world without understanding local circumstances. So I would argue for a more complete globalization of atoms, bits, and people, in ways that are careful, fair, and focused on human development. So "incomplete globalization" is both broken in some ways and incomplete, though my focus is on the ways it is incomplete and imbalanced between globalization of atoms, people, and bits.

You make a productive distinction in the book between Xenophiles and bridge figures. What are the differences between the two? What kinds of functions do they each serve in connecting people together across national differences? How do they both fit within a larger vision of a more cosmopolitan culture?

For me, bridge figures are the cultural brokers and translators who work to make cultures understandable to each other. Bridge figures have deep attachments to two or more cultures – they've usually lived and worked in different parts of the world, and they've chosen to champion those cultures, identifying the good parts in one and introducing them to the other.

If you're going to have an advocate for a culture, they need someone to advocate to. Xenophiles are people who seek inspiration and new ideas in different cultures. They don't have the background in the different cultures to build new bridges, but they can cross the ones that bridge figures build.

For the project of increasing global understanding and connection, both types of figures are critical. I probably emphasize the function of the bridge figure more thoroughly in *Rewire* because it's hard for me to imagine much global connection without bridging. But xenophiles – particularly xenophiles who wear their interests and passions on their sleeves, like Anthony Bourdain and his relentless search for interesting global food – are enormously important in promoting the possibility and importance of international connection. Not everyone can be a bridge figure, I argue – it's an accident of circumstances as well as a choice of perspective and temperament – but xenophilia is a choice, and one I hope more people will make.

What steps might educators take to foster a greater interest in and engagement with the kinds of global communication flows that you value? Is it simply a matter of encouraging Americans to learn foreign languages or beefing up geography teaching, or does it require rethinking the curriculum at a deeper level?

Languages, geography, history, and travel are all powerful tools to encourage engagement, but I think we need a more fundamental change in educational systems. We need much greater awareness of interconnection so that the importance of understanding the wider world is far more apparent. We're lousy about teaching students the complex systems that hold the world together – trade, financial flows, shipping, migration – so it's not a surprise that complex stories that require us to understand interconnection are hard to develop audiences for.

You talk a bit in the book about some of the themes we tackled in *Spreadable Media* – for example, the degree to which more and more media come to us because they are passed along by our friends rather than through mainstream distribution. How does this impact the challenges we face in developing a more "cosmopolitan" perspective on the world? What do you see as some of the limitations of "social discovery?"

I see social discovery as a third paradigm in how we find information online. In the early commercial Internet, we saw a lot of curators from an earlier generation of media taking their place in the digital world. These curators are very helpful in guiding us to unexpected discovery, pointing us to media we might not have otherwise found, but they have been challenged and unseated by an Internet-age suspicion of "gatekeepers," who silence some voices and amplify others.

For much of the development of the consumer Internet, search has been a dominant paradigm. In search, we look for precisely what we want, and we often find it. It's a very rewarding experience, but it's one with some complicated implications. It's possible to surround ourselves with information that confirms our existing biases and prejudices, and to filter out voices that might challenge our preconceptions. And search demands that we know what we're looking for, which is problematic, because we don't always know what we want or what we need.

Social discovery has emerged in part as a way of reintroducing serendipity into online discovery. It gives us signals about what our friends are interested in that we've not yet discovered, which allows us the experience of novelty and discovery. But what we're discovering is what our friends knew, which means our horizons are limited to those of our friends. If we're blessed with a broad and knowledgeable set of friends, this can be a very profound discovery mechanism. But, for many of us, our friends have similar backgrounds and similar perspectives, and discovering the world through their shared media may reinforce our existing worldviews, not only telling us what we want and expect to hear, but persuading us that our perspectives are universal ones, because our friends share that perspective.

I think that spreadable media escape some of these limitations, in that fandoms often bring together people from very different backgrounds around a shared media experience. Sharing a fondness for sumo gives me a point of encounter with people in Japan, Mongolia, Bulgaria, and Brazil (four countries well represented in sumo at present), and the possibility to discover new perspectives through the encounter. But it's possible to imagine other experiences of sharing an interest that leads you back to people you already encounter in your daily existence – I'm not sure my experience as a Red Sox fan broadens my social or global perspectives very much.

You draw heavily across the book on your experiences with Global Voices. What has this project taught you about the kinds of human resources, processes, and technologies needed to facilitate meaningful exchanges across national borders?

Global Voices has taught me two major lessons: the importance of face-to-face relationships, and the idea that cross-cultural communication is a skill. Global Voices is celebrated as a virtual community that somehow manages to bring 1,400 people in 100 countries together to work on a common project. While that's true, the secret of the community is that we invest heavily in face-to-face contact. The project started at a meeting at Harvard, and most of our important decisions have been made when many of us are able to be together in the same space. It's ironic that a project about connection through digital media is so physically mediated, but I think that just reinforces how significant in-person encounter remains in a digital age. I think a lesson learned from our experience is that it can be very valuable to combine short bursts of face-to-face encounters with use of digital media, to prepare for and deepen relationships. We're big fans of introducing people online, bringing them together in person for a few days, then asking them to work together virtually for years at a time.

Most of the people involved with Global Voices are bridge figures, brokering ideas and information between two or more cultures. I'm increasingly persuaded that this sort of bridging is a skillset that can be developed and cultivated. People in our community who are committed to some other form of cultural bridging aside from blogging or writing – living and working outside their home culture, working across different socioeconomic groups – tend to be our strongest and most productive community members. And people who work with us through the years, particularly people who work in different positions within the organization, develop a very strong suite of tools that allow them to mitigate conflicts and build new connections.

As for the technological piece: we're almost luddites at Global Voices. We used IRC for many years for internal conversations, and mailing lists. We're reluctant to embrace technologies until they are very widely usable. But we're starting to make some shifts. GV Faces is my favorite new project – it's a panel discussion on an issue in the news, held via Google Hangouts and recorded for broadcast on YouTube. When we started Global Voices, it was hard to imagine that we'd see technology advance to the point where we could do a global video talking-heads show, but that's where we are, and I'm loving the outcome.

You also draw on your experiences as a fan of certain forms of global pop music. To what degree might music circulate across borders that it is harder for news to cross? Does this movement pose a risk that the music will be exoticized, decontextualized, and misunderstood, or does it potentially spark interests and connections that can lead to thicker forms of communication down the line? Might the same thing be said for other kinds of cultural products – Japanese anime or Bollywood films, for example?

Music is the easiest route into a new culture for me – I've listened to and collected global pop music since my teens, and my first trip in any new city is to the record store. There are many countries where I know nothing about the politics but something about the music. For me, knowing something about a country's music opens me to learning something about the news or the politics – when I follow the rebellion and civil war in Mali, I'm thinking of the wealth of amazing songwriters in Bamako, and about the guitar playing of Tinariwen and other Tuareg musicians.

There's no doubt that music can be a space for appropriation without exploration. I examine Diplo's use of Brazilian dance music in *Rewire* and conclude that he's skating right up to the line, if not crossing it, in his work with MIA. But I also consider how a blatant, naked appropriation – Deep Forest's use of "Rorogwela," a Solomon Islands lullaby, which they repackage as "pygmy music" from the Congo – leads Internet artist Matt Harding[4] to seek out the creator's family in the Solomon Islands and make a deep and significant personal tie. Harding found a piece of music he loved, learned the complicated story behind it, and it ultimately led him to make personal connections behind the music.

I think cultural media like music, movies, and food are often a shortcut around the caring problem. I may know little about the

Uighurs and their ongoing struggles with the Chinese government, but I know – and dig – the music of Zulpikar Zaitov, and so I'm inclined to pay more attention to Uighur news than I otherwise would. I see no reason why this couldn't work around anime or Bollywood, and suspect it probably does ...

Reflections

When Henry last interviewed me, I'd just released my first book, *Rewire: Digital Cosmopolitans in the Age of Connection*. I had hoped to open a conversation with the book about what we wanted social media to be. Almost six years later, that conversation is more pressing than ever, and I fear we're even farther from the conversation I wanted to have.

The core idea that Henry and I explored in this conversation was that social media weren't broadening our picture of the world. Despite the fact that social media made it possible to hear from anyone in the world, most of us were using social media to (re)connect with people we'd met offline, not making new connections online. We explored some of the solutions I'd proposed in the book, including the possibility of using pop culture as a lingua franca to make connections across borders, the role of communities like Global Voices in encouraging xenophilia, and the possibility that social media platforms had a responsibility for the view their users had of the world.

This last idea was wildly radical when Henry and I discussed it. It's now become one of the main themes of discussion around the role of social media in American life. The discovery of campaigns to sway political opinion in the US through social media – both by paid campaign officials and by actors in Russia – has opened dialog about the power and potential danger of social media. Furthermore, the extreme polarization that characterizes contemporary American politics is being traced to social media, which some fear isolates us in mediated echo chambers. It's become trendy to delete your social media accounts, especially Facebook, as a way of protesting against the control asserted by these powerful platforms.

Some of this conversation was already under way when Henry and I spoke. Eli Pariser had published his influential book on filter bubbles (*The Filter Bubble: What the Internet Is Hiding From You* [2011]), and I saw my work, in part, as ensuring that the conversation expanded beyond the idea that we were being isolated by our politics to include the idea that we were being isolated by nationalism. Henry, who has had his world enlarged by meeting with fans around the world, understood the arguments I was making about incomplete globalization – the idea that we have stuff from around the world, but rarely ideas and perspectives – far better than most audiences did.

I regret that we didn't engage more with the idea I was just starting to develop in *Rewire* – the idea that we could ask social media networks to help us have a healthier, more global view of the world. We're seeing many proposals now – not all well thought out – asking social media platforms to take responsibility for ensuring that their users are protected from misinformation and gain access to a wide range of views. While these ideas are admirable, they rarely deal with the core issue that prevents this from happening – the surveillance-based business model that animates tools like Facebook and Twitter.

What I didn't dare say when Henry and I spoke was the idea that I now shout from rooftops: that social media should be public media, much like public radio and television. As Henry and I discuss in this piece, global citizenship demands a picture of the world that both informs and engages. Our current social networks aren't going to lead us to a world where people hear from people they disagree with in their own countries, never mind people across the globe. We need to start demanding social media that help us encounter a full, nuanced picture of the world, and we should be open to paying for such media with taxpayer funds if the markets don't fill the need for the public good of global understanding.

PART II

PARTICIPATORY LEARNING

5

Introduction to Participatory Learning

In 2006, the MacArthur Foundation made a large-scale commitment to support research and interventions at the intersection between digital media and learning. Connie Yowell, who spearheaded this initiative for most of its duration, was determined to build a field around this topic, identifying key thought leaders across disciplines, and forge them into a network that spoke a common language, developed shared models, and could collaborate meaningfully in order to make a difference in the lives of our children. The people represented in this section were among the many I got to know through almost 15 years of engagement with the research community this initiative helped to spawn.

I was honored to be asked by the MacArthur Foundation to write a white paper, *Confronting the Challenges of Participatory Culture*, which helped to frame the initiative in terms of unequal access to the opportunities offered by a more participatory culture, the social skills and cultural competencies required for young people to plug into the networked society, and interventions – inside and outside the classroom – that might start to address what we described here as the participation gap. Mizuko Ito's Digital Youth Project was launched around the same time, representing the other early foundation for the Digital Media and Learning initiative. Ito's team (initially developed in collaboration with Peter Lyman, who unfortunately died early in the process) conducted a large-scale, multi-sited ethnography which documented how young people were currently using new media technologies, and identified the kinds of informal learning which emerged through their everyday use of networked communication. Many things inspire me about the work Ito and her team did, especially the power of their "Hanging Out, Messing Around, Geeking Out" framework. The members of this team have all gone on to remarkable careers, with most of them continuing to push us toward more inclusive and equitable pedagogical practices and educational policies. Ito, in turn, has recently released another important book, *Affinity Online: How Connection and Shared Interest Fuel Learning* (2018), developed in collaboration with a new generation of young researchers, expanding upon some of the core themes discussed in the interview below.

Sonia Livingstone represents an incredible role model for the kinds of interventions a public intellectual might make in public policy debates. She has been fearless in entering often heated arenas – such as the British tabloid press – and exploring taboo topics – such as children's consumption of pornography – that she feels need to be addressed if we are to achieve some balance in our perspectives on young people's actual practices in a changing media landscape. In the interview below, we observe how this balanced, sometimes cautious perspective plays out around a range of specific methodological and policy questions. Many of us sought to minimize talk of risks because of the moral-panic discourse from those seeking to protect youth from exposure to the networked world; Livingstone acknowledges risks even as she speaks about unrealized potentials, both reflecting the affordances of new media platforms. She argues that we should get the facts on what young people were actually doing with new media and, at the same time, be willing to explore how these technologies might be deployed to enhance lives. Her most recent book, *The Class: Living and Learning in the Digital Age* (2016), traces the social networks of youth from a London school across the multiple spaces – from home and peer culture to school – where they conduct their lives.

S. Craig Watkins has directed urgent attention onto questions of racial and economic inequality in regard to access and opportunity within a networked culture. He has become an important advocate for Black and Latinx youth as he documents and critiques the ways schools often discourage and disempower them. When he began doing this work, the digital divide was understood in terms of minority youth falling behind their White counterparts in developing the skills they needed to succeed in the new economy. Yet, from the start, his work questioned this deficit framing, helping us to see that youth of color were themselves innovators, not least as they developed work-arounds to deal with the obstacles put in their paths. In the interview below, we see his initial framing of some of the issues that would drive him to build a research team which would interview more than 300 educators and students in the Austin area, and spend more than a year observing and documenting their lives. The result is a powerful book, *The Digital Edge: How Black and Latino Youth Navigate Digital Inequality* (2018).

James Paul Gee was already a distinguished linguist and educational theorist when he fell in love with computer and video games. He soon began to advocate that educators needed to be playing games, and, through their participation in what had become an everyday practice for most of their students, they would learn new pedagogical practices that would inform their teaching. Unlike many of his contemporaries in the games-based learning movement, he did not necessarily think games should be brought into the classroom, but rather the classroom and its practices might be redesigned to reflect the core principles that enabled games to become such a powerful learning platform. By the time we did this interview, Gee had already written multiple books helping educators understand why video games mattered. Here he sums up the debates around games and learning that had taken shape to a large degree around his work (and that of his students and colleagues). He discussed here a then-recent book he had published with his wife Elizabeth Hays, which used *The Sims* and the fan practices around it to address gender and learning. One of Gee's most lasting contributions to the larger literature on participatory learning has been his concept of affinity spaces, a model that stresses the ways that people come together around shared resources and goals, without necessarily needing to forge strong social ties amongst participants, in order to support informal learning.

My interview with Antero Garcia was conducted upon the publication of his book, *Good Reception: Teens, Teachers and Mobile Media in a Los Angeles High School* (2017). A rising star in the Connected Learning movement, Garcia had been a high school teacher in South Central Los Angeles. He has been able to bring a front-line perspective to helping us understand the ways students and teachers talk past each other where mobile technology is concerned. There were so many moments in this exchange which I found poignant, not the least his response to my request that he imagine he had three wishes with which to transform current schooling practices. I also appreciated his openness in talking about mistakes he made, failed experiments through which his current understanding of these issues takes place, given how fearful academic researchers often are about presenting anything other than an armored self-representation to the world. In my original "Eight Traits" post, I concluded:

> Of these eight traits, the only one which might describe our current educational institutions is "unequal." ... Our schools have not kept pace with the changing environment around them. If we were to start from scratch and design an educational system to meet the needs of the culture we have just described, it would look very little like the current school system. Our schools doubly fail kids – offering them neither the insights they need to avoid the risks nor the opportunity to exploit the potentials of this new participatory culture. Indeed, the skills kids need to function in the new media landscape are skills which are often read as dysfunctional and disruptive in the context of formal education. Kids are, for the most part, learning these skills on their own, outside of school, with the consequence that they are unevenly distributed across the population.

My interview with Garcia brings us back to the ways our schools fail kids and the ways in which opportunities for meaningful participation remain unevenly distributed. These problems haven't gone away. If anything, they are even more entrenched than when I wrote that passage 15 years ago. But people like Garcia are helping to train the next generation of educators and challenge our assumptions about what can be, and is being, done in "urban schools." As he does so, Garcia can build, as he notes, on the work which emerged from the Digital Media and Learning, and Connected Learning, initiatives that MacArthur supported through these years.

References

Garcia, A. (2017). *Good Reception: Teens, Teachers and Mobile Media in a Los Angeles High School*. Cambridge, MA: MIT Press.

Ito, M., Martin, C., Pfister, R., Rafalow, M., Salen, K. and Wortman, A. (2018). *Affinity Online: How Connection and Shared Interest Fuel Learning*. New York University Press.

Jenkins, H., with Purushotma, R., Weigel, M., Clinton, K. and Robison, A. J. (2009). *Confronting the Challenges of Participatory Culture: Media Education for the 21st Century*. Cambridge, MA: MIT Press.

Livingstone, S. and Sefton-Green, J. (2016). *The Class: Living and Learning in the Digital Age*. New York University Press.

Watkins, S. C., Lombana-Bermudez, A., Cho, A., Vickery, J., Shaw, V., and Weinzimmer, L. (2018). *The Digital Edge: How Black and Latino Youth Navigate Digital Inequality*. New York University Press.

Further Reading

For other blog interviews that address questions of participatory learning, see *Confessions of an Aca-Fan* at henryjenkins.org, with: Anne Collier (Jan. 4, 2007); David Williamson Shaffer (Jan. 24, 2007); Lissa Soep (Aug. 19, 2007); David Hutchinson (Oct. 21, 2007); Erin Reilly (Dec. 10, 2007); Eric Klopfer (July 6, 2008); Rebecca Black (Sept.

15, 2008); The Computer Clubhouse team (Dec. 1, 2009); Heather Chapman (Dec. 21, 2009); Global Kids (Feb. 25, 2010); Rich Halverson (March 23, 2010); Jessica Parker (May 5, 2010); Colin Lanksheer and Michele Knobel (May 26, 2010); Ines Dussell (Aug. 30, 2010); Linda Stone (Nov. 19, 2010); John Seely Brown and Doug Thomas (Jan. 19, 2011); Laura Flemming (Jan. 27, 2012); Catherine Belcher and Becky Herr-Stephenson (Feb. 13, 2012); Kurt Squire (March 6, 2012); Collegeology Games (Oct. 29, 2012); Amy Ogata (May 17, 2013); Lynn Schofield Clark (May 28, 2013); Elizabeth Losh (April 23, 2014); Patricia Lange (May 17, 2014); Tessa Johls (Sept. 12, 2014); Howard Gardner and Katie Davis (Oct. 10, 2014); Carrie James (Oct. 17, 2014); Meryl Alper (Nov. 10, 2014); Belinda S. De Abreu and Paul Mihailidis (Dec. 1, 2014); Connected Camps (May 25, 2015); Lisa Guernsey and Michael Levine (Oct. 20, 2015); and Sonia Livingstone and Julian Sefton-Green (June 16, 2016).

6

"Hanging Out, Messing Around, Geeking Out": The Digital Youth Project (2008)

Mimi Ito is a cultural anthropologist, learning scientist, entrepreneur, and an advocate for connected learning – learning that is equity-oriented, youth-centered, and socially connected. She is the Director of the Connected Learning Lab, Professor in Residence, and John D. and Catherine T. MacArthur Foundation Chair in Digital Media and Learning at the University of California–Irvine, with appointments in the Department of Anthropology, the Department of Informatics, and the School of Education. She is also co-founder of Connected Camps, a non-profit providing online learning experiences for kids in all walks of life.

danah boyd is a principal researcher at Microsoft Research, the founder/President of Data & Society, and author of *It's Complicated: The Social Lives of Networked Teens* (2014).

Becky Herr-Stephenson, Ph.D., is a clinical assistant professor in Loyola Marymount University's School of Education. Her work focuses on access and equity in education.

Heather Horst is Professor in Media in Communications at the University of Sydney, interested in the emergence of new mobile media practices across the Asia-Pacific region.

Patricia G. Lange is an anthropologist and Associate Professor of Critical Studies and Visual & Critical Studies at California College of the Arts in San Francisco.

C. J. Pascoe is a sociologist at the University of Oregon, where she researches young peoples' experiences of gendered, sexual, classed, and raced inequalities in school.

Dan Perkel is a director at IDEO, a global innovation and design firm, where he helps lead its media and technology work and design research practice.

Rachel Cody Pfister received her Ph.D. from the Department of Communication at the University of California–San Diego.

Christo Sims is an assistant professor in the Department of Communication at the University of California–San Diego.

Lisa Tripp is a scholar-practitioner of cinema studies and media education at Florida State University's College of Motion Picture Arts.

Can you give us some sense of the scope and scale of your project?

Mimi Ito: This was a study that was conducted over three years, with 28 researchers and research collaborators. We interviewed over 800 youth and young adults, and conducted over 5,000 hours of online observations. This was done in the form of 22 different case studies of youth new media practices. Some of the studies looked at particular online sites, such as YouTube and social network sites. Other studies looked at interest groups, such as gaming groups and fans of anime and *Harry Potter*. Other groups also recruited youth from local institutions such as afterschool programs, parent networks, and schools. We believe that this is the most extensive qualitative study of contemporary youth new media practice in the US.

What were your goals with this project?

Mimi Ito: Our goal was really to capture youth perspectives and voices to understand what is happening in the online world today. We wanted to look at how young people are incorporating new media into their everyday social and recreational lives, in contexts that they find meaningful and motivating. Our thought was that it was only by looking at these kinds of youth-driven contexts that we could get a grasp of what youth were learning through their online participation, and how that activity was changing the shape of our media and communications landscape.

Ethnography often gets praised for its process of discovery. What was the biggest discovery your team made through this process?

Mimi Ito: One of the strengths of the ethnographic process is that it involves listening and learning from people with different perspectives, and having that inform our research frameworks. One of the big things that we learned from doing this with such a large research team was how it was that different kinds of youth practices and social groups were related to one another, either in a synergistic way or in a more antagonistic way. We learned that the main thing that distinguishes different kinds of youth new media practices was the difference between what we call "friendship-driven" and "interest-driven" participation. Friendship-driven participation is what most youth are doing online, and involves the familiar practices of hanging out, flirting, and working out status issues on sites like MySpace and Facebook. Interest-driven participation has to do with more of the geek and creative types of practices, where youth will connect with others online around specialized interests, such as media fandom, gaming, or creative production. It wasn't just the usual things like gender and socioeconomic status that necessarily determined the big differences, but it also had a lot to do with categories in youth culture, like what is considered "cool," "popular," or "dorky."

Heather Horst: In addition to friendship-driven and interest-driven genres of participation, we also identified three genres of participation and learning – hanging out, messing around, and geeking out. Hanging out is when kids are using technologies like IM (Instant Messenger), Facebook, or MySpace to hang out socially with their friends. Messing around is when they are looking around online for information, or tinkering with media in relatively casual and experimental ways. Geeking out is when they really dive deep into a specialized area of knowledge or interest.

What is important about this framework is that it's not about categorizing kids as having a single identity or set of activities. What we are doing is identifying different ways in which kids can participate in media culture, and this can be quite fluid. For example, we talk in our chapter on "Media Ecologies" about a teen named Derrick who participated in Christo Sims's study of Rural and Urban Youth. He uses Instant Messaging and his mobile phone to coordinate hanging out with his friends. Yet – and like many other teens – Derrick has also earned a reputation for geeking out through his interest in locating and downloading movies through BitTorrent. He also uses the Internet to "mess around," such as the time he did a search on Google until he found tutorials and other information to help him build a computer. The diversity of practices reflect differing motivations, levels of commitment, and intensity of use which frame Derrick's (and other youths') engagement with new media ...

Parents often express concerns that young people are interacting online with people they don't know, while those excited about social network sites talk about the ways they allow us to escape the constraints of local geography. Yet your report finds that young people often use these tools primarily to interact with people whom they already know. What can you tell us about the relationship between the online and offline lives of teens?

danah boyd: While there are indeed examples of teens meeting others through these sites, it is critical for adults to realize that these sites are primarily about reinforcing pre-existing connections using mediated technologies. Youth's mobility is heavily curtailed and they desperately want to hang out with their friends from school. These sites have become that gathering space. Just because they can be used by youth to connect to strangers does not mean that they are. By focusing on the possibilities of risk, adults have lost touch with the benefits that these sites afford to youth.

Christo Sims: As danah says, most of our participants used social network sites to complement their offline social relationships, rather than to experiment with identity or to make a bunch of new "friends" from around the country or world. With that said, there were instances where youth developed online relationships that extended beyond schools, neighborhoods, and local activity groups. Youth that were more marginalized in their local social worlds would often go online for friendship and intimacy. We heard several stories of gay and lesbian youth using Internet-based tools in these ways. Similarly, we heard stories of immigrants and ethnic minorities connecting online, despite being widely distributed geographically. Then, there's youth who engaged in interest-driven online participation who often interacted with folks far beyond their local region. When friendships did develop, they grew over sustained participation in those interest-driven activities, not out of more friendship- or intimacy-seeking behavior, as you'd find in an online dating site. Finally, we did hear several stories of youth developing penpal-like relationships with other teens. These interactions tended to be conversational, sharing accounts of what life was like in their respective towns or cities, discussing the challenges and confusions of being a teenager. These sorts of interactions more closely resemble the self-exploration and identity-play that earlier accounts of online participation tended to emphasize – a sense of anonymity, a degree of freedom from the trappings of one's identity in the family or at school – yet they weren't anywhere close to the dominant day-to-day uses of these tools.

Dan Perkel: Just to follow up on a point that Christo alludes to, there are in-between categories of people that might be overlooked in the split between "people you do already know" and "strangers." For example, there are people who are friends of friends, or friends of cousins, who you may not know, but who go to neighboring schools, or live in the same area of town. We heard from participants in San Francisco, the East Bay, and, I believe, in Brooklyn as well – stories of people meeting up and getting to know people who they knew through others but only "met" using MySpace or another site. We also heard stories, or in some cases watched people play out situations, where they had met someone offline and gotten their MySpace username so that they could contact them later. This was one way of facilitating dating (like asking someone for a phone number). In this case, this is someone that they have met, but who is not necessarily someone they "know," or at least have any other contact with, before back-and-forth conversations using social network sites. The point is that we learned how confusing it can be to even categorize who is a stranger versus a known person. How some of the participants use online media happens in the space in-between.

Many writers talk about "digital natives" or describe these young people as "born digital." What do you see as the strength and limitations of these terms, given what you found in your research?

Becky Herr: One potential strength of the term "digital generation" for describing young people and their relationship to technology is its acknowledgment that youth are using media and technology in interesting and important ways. Talking about kids as "digital natives" can be seen as a counterargument to pervasive discourses about kids as deviant users of technology – hackers, cheaters, wasters-of-time – or kids as victims of technology – the "prey" of online predators, for example. This is not to say that the term is used exclusively to describe positive interactions with technology – it also emphasizes the gap between the ways "digital natives" use technology and the ways non-natives (like adults) use technology.

What is worrying about the discourse of digital natives is that talking about young people as a "digital generation" risks romanticizing certain types of youth participation and ignoring important differences in access to media and technology, including barriers to access that are not tied to a lack of hardware – barriers such as not reading and writing in English, being a girl and having to compete with boys in a classroom with limited resources, or parental rules born out of moral panic. Further, the idea of a digital generation marked by shared characteristics (other than the dates of their birth) that outweigh other aspects of identity/subjectivity – race, class, gender, ability (etc.) – is problematic. What we have found in the Digital Youth project is that there is a huge amount of variation in the ways kids are using media and technology in their everyday lives. Yes, the ways in which these practices are enacted vary, often by peer group or by individual kid. We've also found that things like class, race, and gender continue to have significant influence in kids' lives.

In my own research, for example, I worked with kids at the middle-school level who were using media production software (iMovie and PowerPoint) for the first time. At home, most of the students I observed and interviewed did not have a computer, Internet access, or any video equipment. However, they had other media and technology that was incredibly important to them and that they used in creative and sophisticated ways to find information, to express themselves, to communicate with friends, and to mess around in order to figure out things like game cheat codes or how to substitute a borrowed digital camera for an mp3 player. Some had vast music or DVD collections, others spent hours each day playing games on a video game console. Were they "digital natives?"

Christo Sims: There are also plenty of folks who weren't "born digital" who have developed incredible fluency in various forms of online participation. We also met numerous youth who weren't technically adept or comfortable participating online. By emphasizing a generational break, we risk mystifying the factors that structure online participation, and equating competency automatically with age.

danah boyd: Many of those who use these terms often do so with the best of intentions, valorizing youth engagement with digital media to highlight the ways in which youth are not dumb, dependent, or incapable. Yet, by reinforcing distinctions between generations, we reinforce the endemic age segregation that is plaguing our society. Many social and civic ills stem from the ways in which we separate people, based on age. If we want to curtail bullying and increase political participation, we need to stop segmenting and segregating.

Parents and teachers often want to structure young people's time online. Yet your research suggests that some of the most productive experiences come when young people are "hanging out" or "messing around" with computers in relatively unstructured ways. Explain.

Mimi Ito: In a lot of our case studies, we saw examples of kids picking up media and technical literacy through social and recreational activity online. When they were given time and space to experiment, they often were able to pick up knowledge and skills through messing around, whether that was learning how to make a MySpace profile, experimenting with video, or figuring out how to use cheat codes in a game. Some kids used this kind of messing around as a jumping off point toward much more sophisticated forms of creative production, or engagement with specialized knowledge communities.

Christo Sims: One story that comes to mind is that of a youth named Zelan, whom we feature in one of the sidebars in the Work chapter. Zelan comes from a very rural area where most of his peers will end up in working-class jobs, doing construction, building roads, working as mechanics. Zelan, who identifies himself as a computer geek, leveraged his technical know-how for economic gain, starting in junior high school: fixing electronics, buying and selling gaming and computer gear, and servicing the computers of neighbors and teachers. His passion, though, has been video games. He started as a player but soon became an enthusiast, subscribing to game magazines, following the latest releases, looking for tips online. In addition to becoming a fan, he started messing around with broken consoles, taking them apart to see how they worked, trying to fix them so he could play a better console or sell it for a profit. He did all this without seeing it as leading toward a career or success in school. It was only once he started seeing that his gaming interest was actually valuable to others at school and in the community that he began to imagine how these interests could lead to a life after high school. When I first met him, he was a junior and was thinking of starting a computer service business when he graduated. When I saw him again last summer, he was headed to a technical college on a scholarship.

Dan Perkel: Another person featured in one of the sidebars is Jacob. Jacob was an African American senior who had moved from the East Bay to Georgia and back again. Jacob, like others we talked to in our studies, joined MySpace when someone else made an account for him. For a while, Jacob didn't understand how to customize his page – again, like other new members to the site – and had other people do it for him. On the friendship-driven side, he used MySpace as a way to communicate with people he met and friends he left behind after various moves. However, at some point, he made the connection between changing MySpace profiles and the web design classes that he had gotten into at school. He then took the time to better understand how to customize his own profile and considered making and distributing MySpace layouts, something he had seen others do on the site. When I last talked to him, he was considering a career in web design and said he had been offered a job already.

danah boyd: It is important to note that "productive" engagement doesn't necessarily mean only traditional learning or media and technical literacy. As a society, we've never spent much time considering how youth learn to be competent social beings, how they learn to make sense of cultural norms and develop social contracts, or how they learn to read others' reactions and act accordingly. We expect youth to be polite and tolerant, respect others' feelings, and behave appropriately in different situations. This is all learned. And it is not simply learned by kids being told how to behave. They need to experiment socially, interact with peers, make mistakes, and adjust. Stripping social interactions from youth's lives does not benefit them in any manner. I would argue that even the oft-demeaned social practices that take place online are extremely productive ...

You note throughout the report a broadening of who gets to "geek out" in today's youth culture. Explain. What factors are reshaping cultural attitudes toward "geek experiences?" Who gets to "geek out" now who didn't get to do so in the past?

Mimi Ito: Now that digital media and online networking have become so embedded in kids' everyday social and recreational lives, there is a certain baseline of technical engagement that is taken for granted. Only certain kids, though, decide to go from there to what we consider more geeked-out kinds of practices. Predictably, it tends to be boys who geek out more than girls. Even though girls are often engaging in highly sophisticated forms of technology use and media creation, they frequently don't identify with it in a geeky way. What does seem to be changing, though, is the overall access that kids have to more geeked-out practices because of the growing accessibility of digital media production tools, as well as the ability to reach out to interest groups on the Internet. Although our study didn't really measure this, this may be particularly significant for less-advantaged youth who would not otherwise have had access to specialized creative communities or media creation opportunities.

Patricia Lange: Being able to connect with dispersed networked publics enables kids to explore skills and receive mentoring that may be difficult to gain from co-located peers or teachers who do not have the same interests or experiences. For example, in my study of the video-making culture of YouTube, accessing mentors or assistance in a "just-in-time" fashion is inspiring and encouraging, especially given kids' decreasing ability to connect with other adults and potential mentors in neighborhoods and local communities. One of the things we heard very often was that friends, family, and kids at school often did not understand why young YouTubers wanted to "geek out" making videos. YouTube participants' school peers did not always have as much familiarity and expertise with how media are put together as kids on YouTube demonstrated. Many of the kids we interviewed have already had extensive experiences making media. They often have very sophisticated visual literacies and complex ideologies about what makes a good or bad video, what constitutes appropriate participation in technical groups, and how they think about online safety. Failing to engage with these sites in school means there is no hands-on dialog between teachers and students that might help shed light on why some kids thrive by geeking out and why others have difficulty ...

In his recent book *The Dumbest Generation*, Mark Bauerlein writes, "In an average young person's online experience, the senses may be stimulated and the ego touched, but vocabulary doesn't expand, memory doesn't improve, analytic talents don't develop, and erudition doesn't ensue." What kinds of evidence did you find which might support or challenge this assertion?

Becky Herr: I don't think that Bauerlein's claim (as quoted here) is completely off the mark. For many young people, including some of those whom we interviewed and observed in the Digital Youth Project, the Internet is a "vast wasteland" of flash games shrouded by banner ads, websites full of inaccurate information, and corporations looking to make money off young eyeballs. However, unlike Bauerlein, I don't think this is the fault of the kids. I think it's our fault as adults – particularly adults who are parents, educators, and media makers – for not making an effort to understand the Internet from a kid's point of view, and for preventing kids from having the time and space to mess around in ways that encourage them to learn to evaluate what they come across online.

I think what's important to unpack with respect to Bauerlein's claim is that his criticism is rooted in specific, class-based assumptions about media and about childhood. These are not new assumptions, nor are they new criticisms. Similar issues of media damaging young people's hearts and minds have been levied in relation to earlier forms of media. In talking with parents and teachers about our research, I hear echoes of Bauerlein's concerns in their complaints about students writing essays in "IM speak" or eschewing activities parents prefer (for reasons of nostalgia or cultural capital) in favor of playing video games or surfing YouTube.

Mimi Ito: It is tempting to blame the media or a new technology for social or cultural problems. But research has shown that things are much more complex than that, and using media as a scapegoat obscures some of the important underlying issues. A new technology grows out of our existing norms and practices. The fact that many youths cannot escape the culture of distraction that Bauerlein describes is not a problem caused just by the technology, but is much more deeply embedded in, as Becky notes, existing social and cultural distinctions. If kids are doing things online that seem unproductive or problematic, we don't feel that the answer is to ban the media. Instead, we think that it is important to look at and try to shape the underlying social issues. That may be the commercialization of online spaces, lack of connection between kids and teachers, or the fact that academic knowledge seems irrelevant to many kids. It is rarely something that is being driven by the technology alone.

We share a concern about the "participation gap" and how that may create inequalities in experience and knowledge. What obstacles did you discover that might block some young people from exploiting the full opportunities offered by these new media? What role do class differences play in shaping the way young people experience these new platforms?

Lisa Tripp: While young people of all social classes in the US have increased opportunities to go online and use new media, the nature and quality of access still varies greatly. A lot of poor and working-class youth still rely on schools, for example, as their primary source for access to the Internet and digital media production tools. Whereas interest-driven and friendship-driven genres of partici-pation are fundamentally "kid-driven" in terms of growing out of youth interests and motivations, schools typically incorporate media into instruction in ways that are "teacher-driven" and heavily constrained by institutional and adult concerns. This can be seen in many "technology-integrated" assignments that address the standard curriculum without engaging students' interest or curiosity. It can also be seen in school policies and rules that aim to keep out partici-patory media, such as by blocking social network and video-sharing sites, instant messaging, etc. While young people find creative ways to use media at school toward their own interests and goals, those who rely on schools for access to new media are at a disadvantage from other kids. For them, it can be a challenge to find the time, space, and resources to experiment with media in more open-ended ways, and to engage in the media practices that youth tend to find the most meaningful.

In the cases where we interviewed parents, we also saw class disparities in how parents approached computers and the Internet. For the middle-class families in our study (who were also very tech-savvy), parents provided significant scaffolding and encouragement of their children's friendship and interest-driven practices with new media. In contrast, for many of the poor families in our study, the parents had little or no experience with computers (and often learned what they did know from the kids in the family). While in both cases there were opportunities for intergenerational collaboration around the computer, in the case of the middle-class families young people had access to a great deal more support to pursue their own interests online. In the case of the poor families we interviewed, parents wanted their children to focus on using the computer for homework. Many had heard scare stories on the news about MySpace and were hesitant to let their children go online unsupervised. Some parents even took the modem or cable with them when they left their children home alone. This represented a well-intentioned effort to protect children from perceived online risks, but it also made it harder for the young people in these families to mobilize online opportunities. I think these examples speak to the ways in which young peoples' access to new media is determined not just by economic factors, but also social and cultural factors.

danah boyd: In my fieldwork, during the 2006–7 school year, I started witnessing a divide in social network site usage between MySpace and Facebook. While this divide was extremely complex, it can be understood through the lens of Penny Eckert's "jocks and burnouts." These two social network sites became digital turf, and usage reflected social categories. While many teens opted to use both sites, the division that did occur took place along lines of race and class. This may not look like a traditional participation gap as both groups were participating, but divisions in usage that reinforce dynamics such as race and class require us to pause. Consider for a moment that Facebook is the "preferred" tool on most college campuses. What does it mean that some teens are already engaged with the normative collegiate tools, while others are not? How does high school nonparticipation shape early collegiate life?

Your writing is sympathetic to the various ways young people "work around" constraints imposed by adults on their ability to access online social networks. How would you address the concerns of adults who imposed those restrictions in the first place?

C. J. Pascoe: What I tended to see as I studied kids in urban and suburban state schools was that teens constantly tried to work around the constraints the school administration placed on their Internet use. Schools blocked the students' access to Facebook,

MySpace, certain search terms and instant messaging programs. In response, teens developed a sort of knowledge network in which everyone knew which kid could find the proxy servers that would allow them access to these sites (though, of course, none of them knew the name for proxy servers). Interestingly, many of the teachers at these schools found these rules too stringent. One teacher listed off several students who were the proxy server "experts" when one of her students needed to access a forbidden site. Similarly, when one of his students was writing a paper on breast cancer, a teacher let the student conduct research on the teacher's computer because the word "breast" was blocked from the network to which the students had access. In light of these restrictions, it seems that adults are not an undifferentiated mass – that some find certain restrictions of teens' Internet use problematic. It seems that what the more restrictive adults are afraid of is teens' access to information and ability to process that sort of information, as well as the fear that teens might not concentrate on the task at hand – school – if they could be hanging out on MySpace. To those adults, I would say that banning information or certain sites does not prevent teen access. Instead, it creates a community of mistrust. Thus, adults should be working with teens on issues of media literacy, on how to process the sort of information that appears on the banned sites, rather than forbidding teens to visit them.

Heather Horst: We saw parents across the socioeconomic spectrum express considerable concern about the threats and vulnerabilities their kids faced in the contemporary media ecology. Parents worried about the type of information that circulated and, given the timing of our research, the ability of sites such as MySpace to be used as a way to access and exploit their kids. They also worried about multitasking and 'wasting time' online. In addition, because there's fear of kids hanging out outside of the home and their lives can often be overscheduled, young people genuinely felt that they had very little face-to-face contact with their friends. The use of instant messaging and online sites like MySpace, Facebook and so many others is now a part of kids' everyday lives – part of peer culture. In addition, the kids who were doing the most interesting things talked about having (or finding) the time to 'mess around' and explore in a way that did not have 'serious' implications (e.g. being graded). To deny participation in this space is to fail to acknowledge the importance of sociality in kids' lives.

danah boyd: I commend parents and teachers for being engaged and concerned, but I worry that their concerns are often based on inaccurate understandings of danger. As is well documented by researchers at the Crimes Against Children Research Center, the mythical image of the online predator is a completely inaccurate portrayal of the actual dangers youth face online. Yet I found that fear of predators prompted many of the restrictions youth face. When restrictions are driven by fear rather than risk, we do a disservice to our youth. I think that it is very important for parents and other adults to know the data ...

Heather Horst: In addition to knowing the data, as danah suggests, we also want to emphasize that the 'dangers' of online participation must also be understood within the wider context of kids' lives. For example (and to channel C. J. Pascoe), part of the reason going online is so compelling for GLBT teens is that they lack the opportunities for dating that are available to heterosexual teens in their local communities, as well as the social support of other GLBT teens navigating complex relationships. At the same time, the lack of local support from peers, parents, and teachers also makes many GLBT teens vulnerable to individuals who might take advantage of them online. Developing an understanding of these problems from a youth perspective may help to bridge the gap in understanding risk and vulnerabilities – blaming the medium merely distracts us from the root of these complex social problems.

Reflections

The fieldwork for the Digital Youth study was conducted in 2006 and 2007, when MySpace was the dominant social network platform, niche groups congregated on LiveJournal, Twitter and Tumblr had barely debuted, and YouTube was still a novelty. Adults struggled to understand the appeal of social media, and feared that the Internet was a breeding ground for predators. Our research was an effort to help the grown-up world make sense of how and why young people were engaged with new media, at a time when youth online participation was both mysterious and a prelude of things to come.

Today, our digital landscape is occupied by a different set of platforms and players, and concerns have shifted. Tablets and smartphones have raised new concerns about screen time, digital addiction, and technology in the hands of the wee ones. Social and online media have been integrated into our most powerful political and commercial institutions. It now seems quaint to question whether virtual conversations and relationships are "real" or consequential. Instead, we panic over how digital networks are eroding longstanding norms and institutions in both public and private life.

At the same time, many of the underlying dynamics that we identified in the Digital Youth study have withstood the test of time. Young people continue to lead in adopting and testing new platforms and digital literacies, and their elders still fret and complain about them. The genres of participation that we identified – hanging out, messing around, and geeking out – as well as the key distinction between friendship-driven and interest-driven participation still hold in today's digital world. These categories were inherently platform-agnostic, and connected familiar social and cultural patterns that structure young people's lives to new digital practices. And finally, our effort to showcase the diversity in how young people engage with digital life is now more important than ever, as the options for media and platforms continue to proliferate and amplify existing forms of stratification and cultural difference.

The significance of this study has also expanded in unexpected ways in the decade since the book from the Digital Youth study was published. The MacArthur Digital Media and Learning Initiative funded varied programmatic interventions during those years, including YOUMedia, a youth digital maker space at Chicago's Harold Washington Library. The design of the space was inspired by the genres of participation we identified in the book, with areas devoted to hanging out, messing around, and geeking out. Eventually the book title and the genres became an acronym, HOMAGO, as well as a set of design principles for a growing network of YOUMedia spaces in libraries and museums across the country. HOMAGO was also a cornerstone for developing the principles of Connected Learning, which undergirded the work of our MacArthur research network, and a growing movement for mobilizing digital technologies toward the goals of progressive education.

7

Risks, Rights, and Responsibilities in the Digital Age: Sonia Livingstone (2009)

Sonia Livingstone is a professor in the Department of Media and Communications at the London School of Economics and Political Science. She researches children's and young people's risks and opportunities, media literacy, social mediations, and rights in the digital age. Her most recent book is *The Class: Living and Learning in the Digital Age* (2016, with Julian Sefton-Green). A fellow of the British Academy, British Psychological Society, Royal Society for the Arts, fellow and past President of the International Communication Association, and founder of the EU Kids Online network, she leads the projects "Global Kids Online," "Preparing for a Digital Future," and "Children's Data and Privacy Online." See www.sonialivingstone.net.

In the broadest sense, your book urges parents / educators / adult authorities to help young people to maximize the potentials and avoid the risks involved in moving into the online world. What do you see as the primary benefits and risks here?

My book argues that young people's Internet literacy does not yet match the headline image of the intrepid pioneer, but this is not because young people lack imagination or initiative but rather because the institutions that manage their Internet access and use are constraining or unsupportive – anxious parents, uncertain teachers, busy politicians, profit-oriented content providers. I've sought to show how young people's enthusiasm, energies and interests are a great starting point for them to maximize the potential the Internet could afford them, but they can't do it on their own, for the Internet is a resource largely of our – adult – making. And it's full of false promises: it invites learning but is still more skill-and-drill than self-paced or alternative in its approach; it invites civic participation, but political groups still communicate one-way more than two-way, treating the Internet more as a broadcast than an interactive medium; and adults celebrate young people's engagement with online information and communication at the same time as seeking to restrict them, worrying about addiction, distraction, and loss of concentration, not to mention the many fears about pornography, race hate, and inappropriate sexual contact.

Indeed, in recent years, popular online activities have one by one become fraught with difficulties for young people – chat rooms and social networking sites are closed down because of the risk of paedophiles, music downloading has resulted in legal actions for copyright infringement, educational institutions are increasingly instituting plagiarism procedures, and so forth. So, the Internet is not quite as welcoming a place for young people as rhetoric would have one believe. Maybe this can yet be changed!

Risk seems to be a particularly important word for you. How would you define it and what role does the discussion of risk play in contemporary social theory?

I've been intrigued by the argument from Ulrich Beck, Anthony Giddens, and others that late modernity can be characterized as 'the risk society' – meaning that we in wealthy Western democracies no longer live dominated by natural hazards, or not only by those. But we also live with risks of our own making, risks that we knowingly create and of which we are reflexively aware. Many of the anxieties held about children online exactly fit this concept.

My book tries to show how society has constructed an Internet that knowingly creates new risks for children, both by exacerbating familiar problems because of its speed, connectivity, and anonymity (e.g. bullying) and by generating new ones (e.g. rendering peer sharing of music illegal). These are precisely risks that reflect our social anxieties about children's growing independence (in terms of identity, sexuality, consumption) in contemporary society.

As you note, some want to avoid discussion of "risk" because it may help fuel the climate of "moral panic" that surrounds the adoption of new media into homes and schools. Why do you think it is important for those of us who are more sympathetic to youth's online lives to address risks?

I have worried about this a lot, for it is evident to me that, to avoid moral panics (a valid enterprise), many researchers stay right away from any discussion or research on how the Internet is associated not only with interesting opportunities but also with a range of risks, from more explicit or violent pornography than was readily available before, to hostile communication on a wider scale than before, and to intimate exchanges that can go wrong or exploit naive youth within private spaces invisible to parents. I think it's vital that research seeks a balanced picture, examining both the opportunities and the risks, therefore, and I argue that, to do this, it's important to understand children's perspectives, to see the risks in their terms and according to their priorities.

Even more difficult, and perhaps unfashionable, I also think that we should question some of children's judgements – they may laugh off exposure to images that may harm them long-term, for example, or they may not realize how the competition to gain numerous online friends makes others feel excluded or hurt.

Last, and I do like to be led in part by the evidence, I have been very struck by the finding that experiences of opportunities and risks are positively associated. Initially, I had thought that when children got engaged in learning or creativity or networking online, they would be more skilled and so know how to avoid the various risks online. But my research made clear that quite the opposite occurs – the more you gain in digital literacy, the more you benefit and the more difficult situations you may come up against.

As I observed before, partly this is about the design of the online environment – to join Facebook, you must disclose personal information, and once you've done that you may receive hostile as well as valuable contacts; to seek out useful health advice, you must search for key words that may result in misleading or manipulative information. And so on. This is why I'm trying to call attention to how young people's literacy must be understood in the context of what I'm calling the legibility of the interface.

You argue that we should be more attentive to the affordances of new media than its impacts. How are you distinguishing between these two approaches?

Many of us have argued for some time now that the concept of 'impacts' seems to treat the Internet (or any technology) as if it came from outer space, uninfluenced by human (or social and political) understandings. Of course, it doesn't. So, the concept of affordances usefully recognizes that the online environment has been conceived, designed, and marketed with certain uses and users in mind, and with certain benefits (influence, profits, whatever) going to the producer.

The affordances approach also recognizes that interfaces or technologies don't determine consequences 100 percent, though they may be influential, strongly guiding or framing or preferring one use or one interpretation over another. That's not to say that I'd rule out all questions of consequences – more that we need to find more subtle ways of asking the questions here. Problematically, too, there is still very little research that looks long-term at changes associated with the widespread use of the Internet, making it surprisingly hard to say whether, for example, my children's childhood is really so different from mine, and why ...

You begin the book by noting the very different models of childhood which have emerged from psychological and sociological research. How can we reconcile these two paradigms to develop a better perspective on the relationship of youth to their surrounding society?

I hope that the book takes us further in integrating psychological and sociological approaches, for I try to show how they can be complementary. Particularly, I rebut the somewhat stereotyped view that psychologists only consider individuals, and only consider children in terms of 'ages and stages', by pointing to a growing trend to follow Vygotsky's social and materialist psychology rather than the Piagetian approach, for this has much in common with today's thinking about the social nature of technology.

However, this is something I'll continue to think about. It seems important to me, for instance, that few who study children and the Internet really understand processes of age and development, tending still to treat all 'children' as equivalent, more comfortable in distinguishing ways in which society approaches children of different ages than in distinguishing different approaches, understandings, or abilities among children themselves.

One tension which seems to be emerging in the field of youth and digital learning is between a focus on spectacular case studies which show the potentials of online learning and more mundane examples which show typical patterns of use. Where do you fall?

Like many, I have been inspired and excited by the spectacular case studies. Yet when I interview children, or in my survey, I was far more struck by how many use the Internet in a far more mundane manner, underusing its potential hugely, and often unexcited by what it could do. It was this that led me to urge that we see children's literacy in the context of technological affordances and legibilities. But it also shows to me the value of combining and contrasting insights from qualitative and quantitative work. The spectacular cases, of course, point out what could be the future for many children. The mundane realities, however, force the question – whose fault is it that many children don't use the Internet in ways that we, or they, consider very exciting or demanding? It also forces the question 'What can be done?' – something I attend to throughout the book, as I'm keen that we don't fall back into a disappointment that blames children themselves.

As you note, there are "competing models" for thinking about what privacy means in this new information environment. How are young people sorting through these different models and making choices about their own disclosures of information?

There's been a fair amount of adult dismay at how young people disclose personal, even intimate, information online. In the book, I suggest there are several reasons for this. First, adolescence is a time of experimentation with identity and relationships, and not only is the Internet admirably well suited to this but the offline environment is increasingly restrictive, with supervising teachers and worried parents constantly looking over young people's shoulders.

Second, some of this disclosure is inadvertent – despite their pleasure in social networking, for instance, I found teenagers struggle with the intricacies of privacy settings, partly because they are fearful of getting it wrong and partly because they are clumsily designed and ill explained, with categories (e.g. top friends, everyone) that don't match the subtlety of youthful friendship categories.

Third, adults are dismayed because they don't share the same sensibilities as young people. I haven't interviewed anyone who doesn't care who knows what about them, but I've interviewed many who think no one will be interested, and so they worry less about what they post, or who take care over what parents or friends can see but are not interested in the responses of perfect strangers.

In other words, young people are operating with some slightly different conceptions of privacy, but certainly they want control over who knows what about them; it's just that they don't wish to hide everything, they can't always figure out how to reveal what to whom, and anyway they wish to experiment and take a few risks.

You reviewed the literature on youth and civic engagement. What did you find? What do you see as the major factors blocking young people from getting more involved in the adult world of politics?

I suggest here that some initiatives are motivated by the challenge of stimulating the alienated, while others assume young people to be already articulate and motivated but lacking structured opportunities to participate. Some aim to enable youth to realize their present rights, while others focus instead on preparing them for their future responsibilities.

These diverse motives may result in some confusion in mode of address, target group, and, especially, form of participation being encouraged. Children I interview often misinterpret the invitation to engage being held out to them (online and offline) – they can be suspicious of who is inviting them to engage, or quickly disappointed that, if they do engage, there's often little response or recognition; and they can be concerned that to engage politically may change their image among their peers, for politics is often seen as 'boring', not 'cool'.

In my survey, I found lots of instances where children and young people take the first step – visiting a civic website, signing a petition, showing an interest – but often these lead nowhere, and that seems to be because of the response from adult society. Hence, contrary to the popular discourses that blame young people for their apathy and lack of motivation or interest, I suggest that young people learn early that they are not listened to. Hoping that the Internet can enable young people to 'have their say' thus misses the point, for they are not themselves listened to. This is a failure both of effective communication between young people and those who aim to engage them, and of civic or political structures – of the social structures that sustain relations between established power and the polity.

Reflections

Thanks so much for the opportunity to think about how my thinking – and the world – have moved on in the past decade. On re-reading my original interview about *Children and the Internet* (Polity, 2009), I am struck by what hasn't changed as well as what has changed. I say this because my students are always telling me that ten years ago is a long time in this fast-moving, technologically innovative digital age, and that perhaps academic works written so long ago are no longer relevant.

First, it's depressing to realize that, for the past decade, I and many others have been calling on designers, producers, regulators, and technological experts to imagine better how the Internet could serve rather than hinder children's interests, needs, and rights. Now, as then, children are struggling with an Internet made – implicitly or explicitly – for adults, which gives little attention or effort to what might benefit children or advance their best interests.

This means that policy makers, practitioners, and researchers are still in the business of observing children's creative but risky workarounds in their Internet use – and while these are often intriguing, and even admirable, there's still much that threatens their wellbeing. In responding to this, I would reiterate my earlier argument that, rather than restricting children, we should redesign this new environment by learning from the familiar offline environment in its provision of play spaces, public libraries, non-formal learning opportunities, traffic and planning regulation, and diverse means of fostering the civic inclusion of young people.

This is not to say that the latter is in any way sufficient. But at least, offline, child-rights-focused efforts built up over decades, even centuries, mean that we have significant public and civil society institutions effective in supporting children, whereas online these are signally lacking in meeting children's needs. Meanwhile, children's online lives are being rapidly monetized in two ways – via the sizeable market deliberately targeting children, and via the vast, global market blind to the fact that many children fall within its data-scraping grasp.

This leads me to a key change: privacy and data protection. It amazes me that many of us didn't anticipate the importance of personal data in shaping the nature of the digital environment, and, therefore, the prospects for society as global platforms harness the traces of everything we do online through algorithmic processes of agglomeration, calculation, and profiling. In retrospect, we can see that many of the risks and opportunities for children with which I was preoccupied in 2009 were – and are, now, ever more intensely – mediated by data, to the point where children are being 'datafied' from birth. These processes, predicted to be increasingly infrastructural, surveillant, and discriminatory, are largely unregulated, too complex and opaque for the public to understand fully, and incentivized by profit, not human rights – let alone children's.

Such changes – of dominant platforms, opaque systems, globalized experiences – do not shake my faith in children and young people's values or creativity. Nor am I becoming a technological determinist, for these remain profoundly social processes. But I am more committed than I was ten years ago to advocacy in children's interests, seeking to use my expertise as a researcher to support initiatives that prioritize regulation in the public interest, media and digital literacy education of all kinds, and human rights standards and bodies concerned to respect children's rights in the digital environment.

8

Is Facebook a Gated Community?
S. Craig Watkins (2009)

S. Craig Watkins is the Ernest S. Sharpe Centennial Professor and Founding Director of the Institute for Media Innovation at the University of Texas at Austin. He is the author of five books including *The Young and the Digital: What Migration to Social Networking Sites, Games and Any Time, Any Where Media Means for Our Future* (2009), the collaborative *The Digital Edge: How Black and Latino Youth Navigate Digital Inequality* (2018), and *Don't Knock the Hustle: Young Creatives, Tech Ingenuity, and the Making of the New Innovation Economy* (2019).

The Young and the Digital complicates in some important ways the arguments which Robert Putnam makes in Bowling Alone about the impact of electronic media on our social lives. Why did your fieldwork lead you to reappraise Putnam's arguments?

The fieldwork did force me to reconsider some of the more enduring arguments about media, and, especially, the well-traveled *Bowling Alone* thesis by Putnam. From the very beginning of the Web as an everyday tool, researchers have openly speculated about its influence in our social lives. Does the growing amount of time we spend in front of a screen make us more or less social, more or less interested in our friends, neighbors, and the world around us? Putnam's most compelling evidence regarding these questions is based on television.

Among researchers who study TV as a leisure activity, the medium's greatest legacy is how it influences our connection, or lack thereof, to our neighbors, communities, and civic life. Putnam argues that TV-watching comes at the expense of nearly every social activity outside the home, resulting in the erosion of social capital – a sense of neighborliness, mutual trust, and reciprocity that binds people and communities together. The big fear, of course, is that we will all retreat into our own media fortresses, forgoing any valuable social interaction with friends and acquaintances. While I understand the concern, the research evidence simply does not support it.

This was certainly true in our research. As we began talking with young people and combing through our survey results, it became clear that their engagement with technology is, first and foremost, a social activity. Conventional wisdom contends that time spent at home with TV is time spent away from friends and public life. But computer and mobile phone screens represent very different kinds of experiences than the ones traditionally offered by TV. Among the teens and young adults that we talk to, time spent in front of a computer or mobile screen is rarely, if ever, considered time spent alone. Screen time, increasingly, is time to connect with friends and acquaintances.

It's true that connecting via a mobile or Facebook is a different way of bonding, but, as I argue in the book, these practices are expressions of intimacy and community. We tend to get caught up on how much time young people spend with their computers and mobile phones. But what I came to understand is that their true interest is not in the technology per se, but rather the people and the relationships the technology provides access to.

Finally, I believe that young people's move online is also forcing us to reconsider another argument made by Putnam regarding decreasing political participation. The final chapter of the book considers how young people's use of social and mobile media appears to be reversing some of the disturbing trends Putnam documents regarding a once-decisive shift among Americans from political participation – for instance, attending political events, signing petitions, or writing to an editor or politician. While establishing their support for President Obama, young people used Facebook, mobile phones, YouTube, and digital cameras to essentially redefine what electoral politics will look like in the future. Their use of digital media was social, communal, and, in its own distinct way, political.

Throughout the book, you have a good deal to say about the ways digital media are reshaping young people's relations to traditional media, such as newspapers and television. What insight can you offer people working in the television industry about their prospects of attracting or holding the attention of younger Americans?

I'm glad you asked me about television. My interest in young people's engagement with the social Web is driven, in part, by a desire to understand the shift from television to screens that are more social, mobile, and personal. It's a historic shift and one that breaks from a more-than-50-year cultural institution and experience – television as the most dominant screen in our lives.

Our research indicates that, among persons aged 30 and under, television is not the first or most preferred screen in their lives. They are just as likely to view their laptop or mobile phone as their "go to" screen. Young people still watch television but in ways that are quite distinct from previous generations – they watch it while media multi-tasking, on the go, and online. Moreover, kids are being socialized to engage TV in ways that are distinct from the generations that grew up in TV-centric households. These and other changes have forced a group of executives accustomed to the dominance of TV in the household to rethink their business and programming models.

The television industry is diligently trying to avoid what has happened to the pop music and newspaper industry. The TV business is struggling with what most of the corporate media world is struggling with, and that is the question, "Who will control content?" It's a hard lesson to learn, but the rules of engagement really are changing.

It will be really interesting to see what network television looks like in about ten years. There is no doubt that it will look different, but it will largely be outside forces – the ways our viewing and media behaviors shift – that will provoke change: everything from rethinking the prime-time schedule (NBC's decision to decrease scripted dramas, and the impending Leno experiment) to the scaling-back of the up-front presentations that once defined the industry's premium status among media buyers.

The biggest thing that the industry has to realize is that they can no longer control content or our viewing habits like they did in the past. It took a while, but they began putting their shows online and making them available as downloads. Hulu – a network response to the rise of YouTube – has shown signs of early success for long-format online video. But there is still a debate within the industry regarding this question of control. That is, should the network partners in Hulu make their content exclusive or, as some contend, make it available everywhere? I think it's clear that if network TV is to have a meaningful future, it will not only have to permit its audience to access content across multiple platforms but also encourage audiences to shape and influence content, too.

You question the argument that digital media have had an anti-social impact on young people. Are there ways that these new media technologies and practices have made us "too social?"

I think so. Still, I realize that the idea of being "too social" is peculiar. Here is what I mean. The assertion that the Web and mobile phones are making us less social, caring, and involved with others is baffling when you consider the preponderance of evidence that actually compels a substantially different question: is today's "always-on" environment making us too social, too connected, and too involved in other people's lives?

In an "always-on" world, we are constantly communicating with each other via social network sites and mobile phones. It was interesting to learn that part of the initial appeal of Facebook among college students, for example, was the opportunity for constant status updates, as well as the chance to gaze into the backstage world of friends and acquaintances. Young college students consistently made references to what they called "e-stalking" – that is, the degree to which their peers frequently use social network sites to track people's lives, activities, and relationships. Twitter and this idea of what Clive Thompson refers to as "ambient awareness" is another example of a technology that promotes a desire to be in constant connection with others.

In the digital age, the idea of being out of touch or disconnected from family and friends is practically obsolete. No matter where we are – in class, at work, driving, or on vacation – the idea of being connected to our social networks is now a constant opportunity and, quite frankly, a constant challenge.

Rather than worrying about the likelihood of becoming anti-social, I wonder if the reverse outcome – being too social – is a more legitimate concern. Talk to teachers in high school and you will learn that students are constantly connecting via their mobile phones while sitting in the classroom. Talk to university professors and there is a growing belief that students are constantly connecting with each other via platforms like Facebook while sitting in class. Again, it's the idea that we are using these emerging technologies in ways that are inventively social – and, dare I say, excessively social.

What challenges are educators facing as they try to teach the generation which has come of age in the era of Web 2.0?

This is a fascinating question, and, I believe, one of many that we are just beginning to reckon with as educators, researchers, and society. Part of my research included spending some time in the classroom and talking with teachers and school administrators.

What I soon discovered is that they are on the front lines of the move to digital. Teachers face a generation of students armed with more personal media than any other generation. Most teachers will tell you that the trend of permitting students to bring mobile phones, iPods, and other devices to school is a big mistake. Just think. The idea that I would have been permitted to bring a personal media device to school would have been out of the question. But it reveals how our values, behavior, and culture are shifting in the digital age.

The main concern among teachers is the degree of distraction these devices encourage in the classroom. It turns out that parents insist that their children carry mobile phones – easier to communicate and coordinate family schedules that are growing more challenging.

In *The Young and the Digital*, I deal with some of the learning and educational challenges/opportunities posed by digital media. There are two kinds of technologies in today's classroom – technologies that pull students away from the classroom, and technologies that pull students into the classroom. I give some examples of both.

But I am also interested in the social and behavioral challenges educators face in regard to technology. These include issues such as citizenship, community, and helping students and educators make smart decisions regarding their engagement with digital media.

Most schools are being forced to deal with student conflicts that occur online and away from school. More and more, administrators are having to contend with issues like cyberbullying or the circulation of photos that reveal some sort of misconduct. These kinds of issues raise questions about privacy and authority (e.g., when is a student's behavior away from school an administrator's concern?). There are no rule books or precedents for what is happening in the digital world and online lives students build.

I was surprised to learn that many principals are struggling with the online behaviors not only of students, but of teachers also. A growing number of teachers, and practically all recent college grads going into the profession, maintain a personal profile. As you can imagine, this raises many questions about the conduct of teachers away from school. Some teachers "friend" their students in places like MySpace and Facebook, while others vehemently reject the idea. Like the rest of society, schools and the people who run them are learning what it means to "be digital."

Building on work by danah boyd and others, you argue that Facebook has operated not unlike a "gated community" and may directly contribute to racial and class segregation in the online world. How can scholarship on race in the physical world help us to better understand how race operates in the virtual world? What steps should be taken to combat segregation in the online world?

It is easy to get caught up in the wonders of what scholars have variously referred to as "being digital," "life behind the screen," or the "second self." But as the Web has become a more common experience, it has also become a more local experience. That is, we use the World Wide Web to communicate most frequently with our friends, work colleagues, and acquaintances – that is, people we know, like, and trust. To use Putnam's language regarding social capital, we use the Web to "bond" more than "bridge." This is certainly true with race.

When danah distributed her blog commentary about the class divisions in MySpace and Facebook, it struck me as a reasonable and even predictable outcome, especially if you understand that what happens in our lives online is intimately connected to our lives offline. Some Web enthusiasts, however, were either surprised or annoyed by her claims.

But, as your work and that of others shows, there is still a real "participation divide" that creates varying degrees of Internet engagement. No matter whether we are talking about virtual worlds, mobile technologies, or social network sites, race matters in the digital world. Most of the movers and shakers in the branding and marketing of the current-generation Web show little, if any, interest in the social divisions that still mark the digital world. Mentioning the social divisions that are a part of the social Web is pointing out a kind of inconvenient truth. We learned a lot while studying young collegians' embrace of Facebook. In reality, most of us use Facebook to connect to people that we know

– we "friend" friends, not strangers, in our computer-mediated social networks. And who our friends are is usually influenced by race, class, education, and geography.

In examining the hundreds of surveys and one-on-one interviews we collected, my grad assistant and I noticed a strong preference for Facebook among young White collegians, and students more generally, with a middle-class orientation. It was more than a casual preference; it was also an intense rejection of MySpace. Our research found an interesting "racialization" of MySpace and Facebook among young people.

I began reading some of the research on the rise of gated communities in America and found some interesting parallels in the language used by residents living in physical-world gated communities and young White collegians who preferred Facebook (a kind of virtual gated community) over MySpace. They both use words such as "safe," "clean," "private," and "neat" to describe attachment to their communities. They both practice what cultural anthropologists call "gating" – that is, the tendency to build physical/virtual, social, and cultural walls that are exclusive.

I also turned to French sociologist Pierre Bourdieu's work. I've used his work before to think about the kinds of cultural capital that young people accumulate, especially in the places that they create and inhabit, and how it works as a source of power, pleasure, and mobility. But, in this case, I was interested in what Bourdieu refers to as the "distinctions" – that is, matters of taste, aesthetics, and values – that middle-class communities reproduce to maintain social and even physical separation between them and those that they view as below their own social status and class position.

When we began our work, it was common to see college students switch from MySpace to Facebook. Among other things, the switch was also a bid for a social status upgrade, a move up the digital ladder. Today, middle-class students in middle and high school are moving straight to Facebook. Social class distinctions, like everything else in the digital age, are trickling down to younger and younger users.

I was also intrigued by Bill Bishop's "Big Sort" argument. In short, Bishop argues that, starting around the 1970s, Americans underwent a massive social experiment that changed one of the most basic features of everyday life – where and with whom we live. The change in geography, Bishop maintains, is really a sorting by lifestyle. Racial and class segregation have been a fact of American life since the early twentieth century (see Douglas Massey and Nancy Denton's work on residential segregation). But Bishop argues that American neighborhoods are now being stratified along ideological and lifestyle lines – not simply "red" and "blue" states, but even more carefully sorted and homogeneous neighborhoods. There are some interesting parallels in the digital world.

I'm a trained sociologist so I find it quite natural and instructive to look at wider sociological trends to understand what is happening in the online world. I simply cannot separate the two.

Finally, social network sites do not cause racial divisions or the desire for homogeneous online communities. Insofar as what we do online is intimately connected to the lives we lead offline, the fact that a kind of digital sorting is happening is not that terribly surprising. Still, it is striking that, among a generation that played a key role in electing America's first Black president, race plays a crucial role in their use of social network sites and who they bond with online ...

Some of your earlier work dealt with hip hop culture. What similarities and differences do you see between the technological and social practices of the hip hop culture and that you've found in your work on digital youth culture?

I've spent all of my academic career studying young people's relationship to media industries and technologies. The work I'm doing on digital youth culture is greatly informed by my earlier work on hip hop culture.

As you know, there has been a substantial change in the way scholars examine the cultural practices and identities young people produce.

Hip hop, like digital culture, is participatory and performative. Hip hop, like the social media practices of youth today, has always been about young people expressing themselves, building community, while also finding places of leisure, pleasure, and empowerment.

In my book, *Hip Hop Matters*, I wrote a chapter titled "The Digital Underground." It was really an attempt to understand how the Web has become the new town square in hip hop culture – the place to find relevant and urgent dialog about a host of issues facing young hip hoppers. To engage a community of young hip hop enthusiasts about a host of important social issues today, you don't turn on corporate radio or read a corporate-run magazine. You go online.

The innovative use of technology has been a part of hip hop's story from the beginning. That's how everything from graffiti art to mix tapes has been produced, bearing a striking resemblance to the DIY culture of social media today.

My work has maintained a steady focus on understanding the world young people create and inhabit. It's clear that, if you want to understand that world today, you have to dig deep into the digital practices, identities, and communities young people are building. Writing *The Young and the Digital* gave me an up-close look at this world. The book and the blog we will be building is an effort to share what we are learning.

Reflections

One of the most significant changes since our conversation has been the increasing presence and influence of Black and Latino youth in the digital world. In 2010, researchers mostly construed Blacks and Latinos as being on the wrong side of the digital divide – the technology-poor side. No one would have dared to predict that, in just a few short years, Black youth, for example, would be spending more time online than their White counterparts. Among young people, Black youth were the first to adopt Twitter at scale, leading to the rise of expressions like Black Twitter, and the Black Lives Matter movement.

Historically, we have thought about Black youth in the world of tech largely through what I call a "deficit narrative" – that is, the tendency to think about what they lack or do not have, such as computers, home broadband, or access to high-quality tech education. And while those factors still matter, they should not overshadow the resilient ways Black youth have made a space for themselves in the connected world. I call this the "asset narrative." In my latest book, *The Digital Edge*, I focus on what Black and Latino youth bring to their adoption of digital media. Among other things, they bring creativity and agency. In a recent survey that I did with NORC / University of Chicago, it is clear that – compared to young whites, for instance – Blacks feel a greater sense of digital efficacy. They express viewpoints that suggest that they feel empowered through the Internet to express their voice and influence institutional authority. As I reflect back, I do not think I adequately appreciated the agency that young Blacks are cultivating through their engagement with tech platforms. Black youth are not simply trend-followers; they are trendsetters in the social media world. Their use of social and mobile media to produce new forms of civic life and pop culture is a real force to be reckoned with. Just ask the Ferguson police department, or executives in media entertainment.

Finally, much has changed in the world of education and how we think about the future of learning. My research with the MacArthur Foundation and the Connected Learning Research Network suggests that schools are struggling to remain relevant in a society and economy that is rapidly changing. What should schools be doing? In *The Digital Edge*, I argue that schools are crucial resources in the lives of children and teens from resource-poor homes and communities. In our fieldwork in Austin, we found that schools provide these young people access to technology, peers, adults (i.e. teachers, mentors, counselors), and community that support their desire to do interesting things with technology, such as making music, film, and art. But even as Black and Latino students pursue more creative opportunities with technology, they routinely encounter classrooms that are "technology-rich, but curriculum-poor." Most schools have entered the STEM arms race, but most educators still lack a plan or course of action that helps young people become what I call "future-ready." Among other things, future-readiness involves helping young people to think about the Internet, our data-driven world, and artificial intelligence in diverse and creative ways. Schools, especially those charged with educating Black and Latino youth, focus mainly on basic tech skills such as how to search or make a piece of digital art. But the real challenge is helping young people develop the disposition to use tech to intervene in the world. In my book *Don't Knock the Hustle*, I argue that schools would do well to study how young creatives – designers, educators, and social entrepreneurs – are building learning environments that teach young people to act more like designers by imagining a better world and using tech and critical thinking skills to make that world a reality. In short, the future of learning is not about acquiring more technology – rather, it is about developing a generation who use technology to build more equitable and sustainable communities.

References

Watkins, S. C. (2019). *Don't Knock the Hustle: Young Creatives, Tech Ingenuity, and the Making of the New Innovation Economy.* Boston: Beacon Press.

Watkins, S. C., Lombana-Bermudez, A., Cho, A., Vickery, J., Shaw, V. and Weinzimmer, L. (2018). *The Digital Edge: How Black and Latino Youth Navigate Digital Inequality.* New York University Press.

9

How Learners Can Be On Top of Their Game: James Paul Gee (2011)

James Paul Gee is the Mary Fulton Presidential Professor of Literacy Studies and a Regents' professor at Arizona State University. He is a member of the National Academy of Education, and a fellow of the American Educational Research Association. He received his Ph.D. in Linguistics from Stanford University in 1975.

We've both been involved in thinking about games and learning for the better part of a decade. What do you see as the most significant breakthroughs which have occurred over this time?

The breakthroughs have been slower in coming than I had hoped. Like many new ideas, the idea of games for learning (better, "games as learning") has been often co-opted by entrenched paradigms and interests, rather than truly transforming them. We see now a great many skill-and-drill games – games that do in a more entertaining fashion what we already do in school. We see games being recruited in workplaces – and lots of other instances of "gamification" – simply to make the current structures of exploitation and traditional relationships of power more palatable. We will see the data-mining capacities of games and digital media in general recruited for supervision, rather than development. The purpose of games as learning (and other game-like forms of learning) should be to make every learner a proactive, collaborative, reflective, critical, creative, and innovative problem solver; a producer with technology, and not just a consumer; and a fully engaged participant, and not just a spectator, in civic life and the public sphere.

In general, there are two "great divides" in the games and learning arena. The two divides are based on the learning theories underlying proposals about games for learning. The first divide is this: on the one hand, there are games based on a "break everything into bits and practice each bit in its proper sequence" theory of learning, a theory long popular in instructional technology. Let's call this the "drill and practice theory." On the other hand, there are games based on a "practice the bits inside larger and motivating goal-based activities of which they are integral parts" theory. Let's call this the "problem-and-goals-centered theory." I espouse one version of this theory, but, unfortunately, there are two versions of it. And this is the second divide: on the one hand, there is a "mindless progressive theory" that says: just turn learners loose to immerse themselves in rich activities under the steam of their own goals. This version of progressivism (and progressivism in Dewey's hands was not "mindless") has been around a great many years, and is popular among "mindless" educational liberals. On the other hand, the other version of the "problem-and-goals-centered theory" claims that deep learning is achieved when learners are focused on well-designed, well-ordered, and well-mentored problem solving with shared goals – that is, goals shared with mentors and a learning community.

As in so many other areas of our lives today, the conservative version (drill and practice) and the liberal version (mindless progressivism) are both wrong. The real solution does not lie in the middle, but outside the space carved up by political debates.

What do you think remain the biggest misunderstandings or disagreements in this space?

Much of what I discussed above is really not about misunderstandings, but about disagreements and different beliefs and value systems, or, in some cases, different political, economic, or cultural vested interests.

The biggest misunderstanding in the case of my own work has been people saying that my work espouses games for learning. It does not, and never has. It espouses "situated embodied learning" – that is, learning by participation in well-designed and well-mentored experiences with clear goals; lots of formative feedback; performance before competence; language and texts "just in time" and "on demand"; and lots of talk and interaction around strategies, critique, planning, and production within a "passionate affinity space" (a type of interest-driven group) built to sustain and extend the game or other curriculum. Games are one good way to do this. There are many others.

The biggest misunderstanding in general is that technologies (such as games, television, movies, and books) are good or bad. They are neither. They are good, bad, or indifferent, based on how they are used in the contexts in which they are used. By themselves, they are inert, though they do have certain affordances. Games for learning work pretty much the same way as books for learning. Kids learn with books or games (or television or computers or movies or pencils) when they are engaged in well-designed and good interactions with adults and more advanced peers – interactions that lead to problem solving, meta-critical reflection, and connections to the world and other texts and tools. They learn much less in other circumstances. But we must humbly admit that humans have never yet found a technology more powerful than print. The number of people who have killed others or aided them in the name of a book (the Bible, the Koran, *The Turner Diaries*, *Silent Spring*) is vastly larger than those who have killed or helped in the name of a game, movie, or television show. Of course, this may change, but it does little good, in the interim, to pretend books are benign, but games are inherently perilous ...

I see game design and learning design (what a good professional teacher does) as inherently similar activities. The principles of "good games" and of "good learning" are the same, by and large. This is so, of course, because games are just well-designed problem-solving spaces with feedback and clear outcomes, and that is the most essential thing for real, deep, and consequential learning. These principles include (among others): making clear what identity the learning requires; making clear why anyone would want to do such learning; making clear how the learning will function to lead to problem solving and mastery; making the standards of achievement high and clear, but reachable with persistence; early successes; a low cost of failure that encourages exploration, risk-taking, and trying out new styles; lots of practice of basic skills inside larger goal-based and motivating activities; creating and then challenging routine mastery at different levels to move learners upwards; using information and texts "just in time" and "on demand"; performance before competence (doing as a way of learning and being); getting learners to think like designers and to be able themselves to design; encouraging collaboration and affiliation with what is being learned as part of an identity and passion one shares with others; good mentoring by other people, as well as smart tools and technologies ...

Women and Gaming: *The Sims and 21st Century Learning* moves us from a focus on the kinds of learning which occur inside the game, as we play, toward the kinds of learning which takes place around the game as people build upon it, through the mechanisms of what you would call affinity spaces or what I call Participatory Culture. You describe this as "gaming beyond gaming." What has motivated this shift of emphasis?

... My focus of late on passionate affinity spaces was caused by the influences of my son Sam (who claims correctly to have taught me everything I know about games), Betty's wonderful work on her tech-savvy girls' clubs, and, of course, you.

The first thing I ever wrote on passionate affinity spaces was motivated by a request that I write a paper about my take on "communities of practice," a notion that has become very popular in a great many areas. In my view, this powerful notion has become attached to so many different things that it is in danger of losing any real meaning. When talking about such notions, I think it is necessary to name what you mean very specifically and name it in such a way that it clearly indicates what you value. This is what you have done with "participatory culture" and what I did with "passionate affinity spaces."

So why did I choose that term? First, I wanted to argue that "interest" gets someone in the door, but not out the door to any deep place unless it leads to lots and lots of practice, and persistence past failure. To get such practice, and persistence past failure, an interest has to be kindled into a passion, and an affinity space needs to be organized to help people to do this.

I use "space" rather than "community" because the word "community" carries a rather romantic connotation which it should not have. I also use the word "space" because the notion of "membership" is very complex in modern Internet spaces. People are "in" the space even if they are just lurking, but what makes them "members" is a much harder and, in some cases (though not all), a more flexible and fungible notion.

Passionate affinity spaces tend to follow the Pareto Principle (20% of the people produce 80% of the outcomes, 80% produce 20% of the outcomes), while school classrooms tend to follow (enforced) bell curves. I want to stress not just multiple forms of, and routes to, participation, leadership, and mentorship in passionate affinity spaces, but also the opportunity for all people in the space to become producers, designers, and creators, as well as mentors to others.

All passionate affinity spaces are organized first and foremost around a specific passion that is not necessarily shared by everyone (some only have an interest), but is the "attractor" in the space around which norms, values, and behaviors are set. The book *Women and Gaming* is about different forms passionate affinity spaces can take, and some forms we applaud. The form we applaud most is not age-graded (young and old are together); allows newbies and experts to be together; and engages in supportive interactions because people in the space accept a theory of learning that says that expertise is not in a person but in the affinity space, and that, no matter how good you are, there is always something more to learn and someone else from whom to get help and mentoring.

Tell us more about the tech-savvy girls' (TSG) clubs. What were the goals behind this initiative? How did these experiences inform *Women and Gaming*?

The following is from Elizabeth Hayes:

> TSG grew out of my interest in differences among how girls and boys engage with gaming more broadly. Not only do girls and boys tend to play different sorts of games, they also do different things with games. In particular, boys are much more likely to mod games, to create content for games, and otherwise to engage with games and other gamers in ways that support their development of technical skills and identities as content creators. *The Sims* is one of few games in which girls and women actually predominate as content creators and modders.
>
> I wanted to give girls who otherwise would not participate in such practices greater access, social support and encouragement to participate. We started TSG, though, with a pretty limited understanding of the learning that takes place through fan communities, or affinity spaces. We initially saw fan sites as sources of information (i.e., tutorials, examples of content) rather than as spaces where the girls could develop identities, interact with other players, and be mentored (as well as mentor others).
>
> A crucial turning point in our perspective was conducting interviews with adult women content creators, described in chapter 5 of the book. These women kept pointing back to the Sims player community as crucial to their interest in content creation and modding, as well as to their mastery of technical skills. Talking to these women made me realize that I had started TSG with a deficit perspective towards women's gaming practices. That is, I'd assumed that we needed to help girls engage in modding practices similar to what boys are doing, rather than starting with an appreciation for what women were already doing.
>
> This change in perspective led us to further investigations of the fan practices already taking place around *The Sims*, and this research

became a very important component of our work. One of my research assistants is just completing her dissertation on *The Sims* Writers' Hangout, a site where players post and discuss *Sims* stories, a form of multimodal storytelling that requires composing images in the game and combining them with often lengthy narrative texts. Another student is investigating the learning of specialist language that takes place in *Mod The Sims*, another fan site devoted to game modding.

This is why discussion of the social spaces around *The Sims* is so central to *Women and Gaming*. We wanted to help others see that what women are doing with games is already exciting and important, and also to shift the lens a bit, in order to encourage people to look at male-dominated game spaces in new ways.

A key theme running through the book is the importance of becoming a designer, rather than simply being a player of games. What accounts for the growing emphasis on design literacies in the twenty-first century?

I think that the importance of design, design thinking, and design literacies today follows from the shape of the world. We live amidst complex systems of all sorts, systems which are risky and dangerous and which interact with each other to create yet more risk. Furthermore, such systems are rarely now just "natural" or just "human made."

I live in Sedona, Arizona. Sedona is a desert. Like deserts from time immemorial, Sedona is cold at night even if it is hot in the day-time. This is not so for Phoenix, which is also a desert. It is hot at night when it is hot in the day-time. This is so because of a heat-island effect. The massive amounts of concrete in Phoenix absorb the heat all day and radiate it out all night. So the temperature in Phoenix is a joint venture of "Mother Nature" and humans.

Solutions to problems involving complex systems demand multiple sorts of pooled expertise, including even the wisdom of crowds. Single-minded, single-focused experts are dangerous, since they undervalue what they do not know and their actions can and do create massive unintended consequences when they intervene in complex systems (as we found out in the 2008 worldwide recession and as Alan Greenspan pretty much admitted in front of Congress).

So people – citizens – need to learn to think of systems as designed, or as things that act like they are designed. They need to know how to produce designs themselves as "models" to think with (and model-based thinking is the core of science).

The United States today is politically polarized and comes at all problems as if they are political or ideological, when in fact most of our problems are complex, the solutions to them are going to be compromises with trade-offs, and we need to continuously question our expertise, values, and goals. We are so polarized today that a core goal of schooling, in my view, ought to be teaching kids to see arguments as designed and as inherently connected to evidence and perspectives and not just ideology, self-interest, and desire.

Of course, the focus on design has also come about because so many digital tools – and other tech tools – developed by and for professionals can be used today by "everyday people" to design, build, and create for themselves. There has always been the danger with any technology – most certainly including books – that people will get divided into two classes: "priests" who are experts and know the deep secrets inside the technology (or make them up), and the "laity" who consume the technology, but do not understand it enough to transform it. The potential of much digital learning today – as well as many passionate affinity spaces – is to allow more and more people to be priests. But this sort of potential has always in human history been opposed and resisted by elites, who always seek to constrain and tame it.

The part of your arguments for affinity spaces which get the most push-back from my students are your claims that "a common passion-fueled endeavor – not race, class, gender, or disability – is primary." To many, this seems like a very utopian claim for these spaces, which you have been careful to describe as not

"communities" in the way that term is most often used. Yet, surely, inequalities impact participants at all levels, from access to the technology, to access to basic skills and experiences, to access to the social networks which support their learning. How can we address these very real inequalities while recognizing that there are indeed ways where class, race, and gender matter differently in the kinds of spaces you are describing?

The statement that passionate affinity spaces are focused on a shared passion (and shared endeavors and goals around that passion) and not race, class, and gender (while allowing people to use such differences strategically as their own choices) is not an empirical claim, it is a stipulation. Something is not a passionate affinity space if it does not meet this condition. So, perhaps there are none. But, then, such spaces become a goal and an ideal and we can talk about how close or far away from that goal and ideal we are.

On the other hand, it does little good to follow the standard liberal line that race, class, and gender are always and everywhere one's determining identities. This, for example, locks an African-American child into always being "an African American." A White kid can be a "*Pokémon* fanatic" or an expert modder, but the African-American kid is always "an African-American Pokémon fanatic" or an "African-American modder."

We are never – none of us – one thing all the time. Sure, the world continuously tries to impose rigid identities on all of us, all the time. But it is our moral obligation – and one necessary for a healthy life – to resist this and to try to create spaces where identities based on shared passions or commitments can predominate.

In reality, the real identities that count in life most – that define us and make us who we are – are rarely named. They are identities like "a person who would never kill someone because they did not share his or her religion" or "a person who would rather love and be loved than be rich" and a great many more such as these. These sorts of identities constitute our most significant form of human sharing and bonding.

And such identities are where the deepest divisions among people occur.

It may be here that I diverge from some others. I have repeatedly seen people who are pissed off because someone said they or their work were not "mainstream." If someone called my work "mainstream" or called me "mainstream," I would be insulted. If I discovered that my work or myself was "mainstream," I would retire or find something else to do. Note, by the way, that NO good academic wants to be mainstream. If something – say, what they teach in high school – is called "mainstream history," you can bet no good young historian wants to do it, and you will find next to no one, old or young, in a good history department with such a sign on his or her door.

Chibi-Robo!, *ICO*, *Psychonauts*, and *Shadow of the Colossus* are not mainstream games. They are, however, great games, and their designers will be long remembered when many mainstream designers are long forgotten. Remember, too, that nineteenth-century America had only two world-class poets (Emily Dickinson and Walt Whitman) and, at the time, neither was remotely close to mainstream. One never published, and the other published his own book himself and reviewed it under various names. The monk Mendel wanted to be a high school biology teacher, but he failed his state teacher's test and was relegated to the monastery's garden. He was unknown in his time, entirely non-mainstream, and yet also the only man in his time who actually knew biology (including Darwin, who knew less than nothing about genetics), though no one knew that until much later ...

Many of the projects coming out of the MacArthur Digital Media and Learning Initiative embrace the importance of passion-driven or interest-driven networks. Yet, increasingly, we are being asked to think about young people who do not have or have not yet discovered driving passions of the kinds the book discusses. How do you respond to critics of "geeking out" as an educational ideal? What can we do for kids who "just don't care?"

A person who cannot find a passion is going to be in trouble in our modern world as far as I am concerned. Many people will gain status, respect, control, and creativity off-market (since not everyone can gain these things on-market for profit, in a world where, in developed countries, only one-fifth of people will be well paid). But all people need to gain these things.

All our schools and institutions are set up very poorly to help kids find their passion. We want to teach "what every citizen should know" in things like science and math (and we succeed: all Americans pretty much know the same things about science, mathematics, and geography – which is nothing).

We think we can force people to learn things. We treat collaboration as cheating. We do not give kids the time – or places where the cost of failure is low – to try out a variety of interests and identities in an attempt to discover passion or passions. We do not let kids engage with professional-like tools and activities in areas such as urban planning, game design, or journalism.

Rather, we define everything to be learned in terms of content names like "algebra" or "civics," even when this "content" might be best learned as a tool-set for other activities like 3-D design. We let rich kids experience what passion and practice can bring one in the world and what the routes to success are, but we do not let poor kids have this knowledge. We treat certifications and degrees as more important than actual talent and achievements.

So what about people who just "don't care?" Barring serious illness, there are none. Every baby is born as a passion-seeking being. That is why children acquire their native languages and master much of their cultures without formal schooling.

One day, when my son Sam was a mere toddler, I found some plastic figures at the grocery store. I had no idea what they were. I brought a couple home and gave them to Sam. They were Pokémon and they led to interest, passion, and practice that made him a passionate gamer. That passion for gaming led, in ways no one could have predicted, to his current passion for acting and theatre, on the one hand, and for

Africa, on the other (since *Age of Mythology* hooked him on mythology, and then on cultures beyond his own).

School is defined around outcomes it knows in advance, but for many children does not meet. Real learning kindles passions that make new kinds of people – and people capable of making themselves over again when they need to – but does not know or predict the outcome, and does not, by any means, insist on the same outcomes for everyone.

Despite your book's title, you spend less time here talking about "gender" than might be expected from other books which talk about women and gaming. What roles does gender play in your analysis? What claims are you making about the different kinds of experiences and identities female players construct around games?

For me, the book is not about gender. It is about women and girls who take gaming beyond gaming to become designers within well-designed passionate affinity spaces that change their lives and the lives of others. It about these women and girls because we believe that what they are doing, how they are doing it (e.g., combining technical modding with modding for emotional intelligence and social interactions), and what they are accomplishing is on the cutting edge of where all of us are going – male or female.

Women and girls are leading the way here as they are in many other areas of society. There has been lots said about modding for games like *Half-Life* and its connections to technical skills – and, indeed, this is important. But much less has been written about modding *The Sims* to create challenges and gameplay that are simultaneously in the game world, in the real world, and in writing things like graphic novels.

Such modding is the force that sustains a passionate affinity space that builds artistic, technical, social, and emotional skills. We wrote the book because these women and girls rock, not because they are women and girls.

Also, I had a sin to expiate. I had left *The Sims* and women gamers pretty much out of my first book on games. Betty helped me see that

The Sims is a real game and a very important one because it is a game that is meant to take people beyond gaming. She helped me see that how women play and design is not "mainstream" (see comments above) but cutting-edge, the edge of the future. If it were leprechauns that were the cutting edge of the future, I would have written about them ...

I know you have expressed in the past great skepticism that our current schooling system can adjust to the potentials of this more participatory culture. Without school involvement, how do we insure a more equitable access to the kinds of formative experiences you describe in the book? On the other hand, how does a school culture so focused on standardized processes and measurements maintain anywhere near the flexibility to respond to personal passions that you've identified in *The Sims*?

What I have called "situated embodied problem-focused well-designed and well-mentored learning" will either come to exist primarily for elites who will get it 24/7 on demand across many institutions and their homes, or it will be given to everyone.

In the first case, the regular ("mainstream") state school system will continue to teach the basics accountably and will exist to produce service workers. In the second case, we will have to reinvent a public sphere and transform our view of society, civic participation, markets, and what constitutes justice, fairness, and a good life. We are headed the first way right now, but there is always hope for the future. Both you and I are trying to push the train to the second future and not the first, though, in the end, in the future the real actors and activists in this "game" will be younger (and often browner) than we are.

The current accountability regime MUST be removed. It is immoral, stupid, and counterproductive. We define accountability around teachers failing to teach children. This is like doing accountability for surgeons by waiting to see how many people they kill and then getting rid of them if they kill too many.

Far better to have accountability back when teachers and surgeons were trained, which means radical changes in schools of education and universities. Surely, we should not wait to see how many patients they kill or kids they screw up. Teachers are punished if a kid's test scores go down, but scores could go down for many reasons, not just what the teacher did in one year. This is like punishing a surgeon when a patient dies in back surgery because his wife poisoned him – and lots of things are poisoning our children: not, by any means, mostly teachers.

What we need accountability for is curriculum and pedagogies, not teachers per se (who should have been well trained and then held to high standards that most of them can and do meet, as in the case of surgeons). Today, curricula and pedagogies are often politicized, seen as right-wing or left-wing. If we could agree on a common measure (say an NAEP [National Assessment of Educational Progress] test, or some other test we can come to agree on), a measure that is given to a sample of students (not given to all), so that it cannot be taught for, then we could simply say which curricula and pedagogies correlate with strong or weak results on the common measure. This is what we do with drugs and surgical procedures.

In the end, though, we MUST change our assessment system or we will never have new learning, since assessment systems, in an account-ability regime, drive what is taught and how it is taught. Today's games and other digital media allow for learning to be so well designed that finishing the "game" means you have learned and mastered what is being "taught." No one needs a *Halo* test after finishing *Halo* on the hardest setting, and no one should need an algebra test after finishing an equally well-designed algebra curriculum.

Furthermore, games and digital media can collect, mine, and artfully represent copious moment-by-moment data on a great many variables. So we can, with such data, assess learning across time in terms of growth; we can discover different trajectories toward mastery and use this information to help learners try new styles; and we can compare and contrast learners with thousands of others on hundreds of variables tracked across time (as we already do with *Halo*, for instance).

When the day comes where we can contrast such assessments (based on growth, trajectories, multiple variables represented in ways that inform and develop learners, and comparison among thousands of people sorted into a zillion different types for different purposes) with our now standard "test score" – one number taken on one day – the game will be over. The choice will then be stark. Either we will develop only some or we develop everyone. The bell curve will be gone. No one needs always to be "in the middle" ("mainstream"). Everyone can, in some places and at some times, be at the very top of their game.

Reflections

I got into video games in 2001 when I was 53 and my son was 6. We played *Pajama Sam* together and I wondered what an "adult" video game would be like. I got one and quickly learned two things: first, that I had ceased to be a good learner, not having been challenged to learn something entirely new – and fail and fail – for a long time; second, that my theories of learning and literacy were ok, but too tepid, too limited, and too untied to the real world (yes there is one, no need for scare quotes). My theories and I were in need of a jolt.

Lots of new science has told us what sorts of creatures we humans are, and told us, too, how, as such creatures, we can live joyously and learn, or suffer and die. Human institutions and society are very poorly set up, indeed, for human flourishing. New and current work on evolutionary biology has illuminated how nature designs human learning, and how humans are designed to re-tool nature for yet better teaching. Teaching and learning in nature are a dance across time, and time scales.

Humans learn from well-guided embodied experiences in the world where something or someone guides their attention amidst the overwhelming buzz of details that are part and parcel of any experience in the real world. They learn best from experiences where they have a goal they emotionally and socially care about, a goal that they may very well be taught to rethink. Humans generalize bottom-up from concrete experiences and need lots of well-guided goal-oriented experiences – and practice – and dialog – to generalize fruitfully.

For humans, the best teacher has and always will be embodied social experiences where the human is face-to-face and in mutually guided dialog with mentors, peers, things, tools, other living things, and the ground. But if we are given this – and we must be given it to thrive – we humans can go yet further. We can save ourselves from our ingrained greed and short-sightedness. We can save ourselves and our imperiled world by making for ourselves, with our best tools, well-mentored, goal-based, emotion-driven experiences that we could never ever have had in life.

Our human stupidity, which is close to destroying the world, is due to the fact that we are creatures who live at a certain spatial and temporal scale. We cannot feel, see, and empathize with the very big and the very small; we cannot see the agency of objects, the mindful groundedness of non-human animals, or the myriad workings of chance.

Video games can be, when they are at their best, a new store of human memory. Human long-term memory is not really about the past. It is not even a good record of the past, since humans change their memories every time they use them. Humans use their memories to plan for the future, to prepare before they act and suffer the consequences, and to make sense of it all and learn "from history" as they say. Human memory (unlike computer memory) is future-oriented, not past-oriented. Video games – like books, movies, music, and dance – can be ways to prepare for the future.

Video games can be particularly good at "mimicking" embodied emotionally driven experiences of action and problem solving for enlightenment, growth, and new possibilities. But not without two things: good mentors, and a return – every so often – to the ground of earth and dialog, our original and ever-lasting home, if we are to survive as humans.

10

Teens, Teachers, and Mobile Tech: Antero Garcia (2017)

Antero Garcia is an assistant professor in the Graduate School of Education at Stanford University, where he studies how technology and gaming shape both youth and adult learning, literacy practices, and civic identities. Prior to completing his Ph.D., Antero was an English teacher at a public high school in South Central Los Angeles. Based on his research focused on equitable teaching and learning opportunities for urban youth through the use of participatory media and gameplay, Antero co-designed the Critical Design and Gaming School – a public high school in South Central Los Angeles. Antero received his Ph.D. in the Urban Schooling division of the Graduate School of Education and Information Studies at the University of California–Los Angeles.

For me, one of the real strengths of *Good Reception* is the perspective you bring as a classroom teacher who worked in South Central Los Angeles. Can you share with us how those experiences shaped the perspective you adopted in this book?

The school at the heart of *Good Reception*, which I call South Central High School (SCHS), was my professional teaching home for eight years. Like many of my teaching colleagues who went through the UCLA Teacher Education Program, I was intentional about rooting myself in a specific school and its community for my career. Long before the events described in *Good Reception*, I'd spent countless hours working alongside students, teachers, and parents in this community. At the same time, I'd been growing increasingly frustrated with the lack of support for teachers as intellectuals, leaders, and transformative agents in the LA public schooling system. I am being a bit dewy (*Dewey*?!)-eyed, I recognize, in centering educational equity in the work and friendships I experienced while at SCHS.

This preamble actually gets to the heart of how I ended up in a doctoral program and conducting the dissertation research that would ultimately find its way into the pages of *Good Reception*. One year, the principal at the school at the time (one of eight I would work with) announced he had completed his doctorate, and the shift from addressing him as "Mister" to "Doctor" was a sudden and intense one. As a teacher – particularly if I was called into his office with my union representative for various challenges – the title change was one to further elucidate who wields power in schools. In what was – in retrospect – a foolhardy decision, I ended up enrolling in a doctoral program in order to increase the social capital of teachers in my school. Of course, I didn't realize this decision would professionalize me into a different set of interests related to research and advocacy at the higher education level.

Related to the story above, part of my push in describing my experiences at SCHS is to disrupt the traditional assumptions about what "urban" schools look like and the kinds of stereotypes associated with our students. The true challenges that persist in this school space – dropout rates, localized contexts of violence and lack of vital resources such as groceries, healthcare, and jobs – are entirely systemic; the generations of willful neglect that have let spaces like SCHS languish do not mean that the students in these schools are any less brilliant or willing to engage in the transformative and democratic purposes of schooling. If anything, as I discuss later in our conversation and in my book, teachers, administrators, and school policies get in the way of the innovative learning principles and ideas of the students at these schools.

You compare your success using mobile technologies in a specific classroom setting with what is now seen as the systemic failure of the LA Unified School District's (LAUSD's) billion-dollar initiative to incorporate iPads into their teaching. What do we learn by comparing these two examples?

Well, the short answer is that we both screwed up. Expanding: we both screwed up in similar ways by trying to blindly reinforce adult power with tools that are inherently about democratized participation and engagement. As my colleague Thomas Philip and I wrote[5] shortly after the LAUSD debacle, no one should have been surprised by the fact that students hacked their devices and used them in ways adults didn't intend. (What surprised us was that it took days instead of hours.) Similarly, as an eager doctoral student ready to dive head-first into my own research, I ignored the tacit knowledge I'd known as a teacher for years: students are way, way smarter than school systems tend to give them credit for. Just as teachers are good at enacting what school is supposed to look and feel like, students, too, participate in the dance of *doing* school without necessarily gaining a whole lot of useful stuff in the process. This is a shame and my use of technology in this study was – initially – complicit in such a cyclical process.

For those who haven't read the book, I should explain that I tried to control what apps and media students could put on the mobile devices they used in my classroom. It didn't work. In the matter of a day, students joyfully played games and listened to their own curated music on the devices I provided them. And this is a good thing. In other research, Thomas Philip and I have seen how mobile devices that lack the social ties and meaning of students' own phones cease to be very useful and, in one example, mainly stayed in students' lockers so that they didn't get damaged. Devices that lack the personal value we typically place on our own mobile phones become more burdensome than educationally expansive. I know this is a lesson I learned quickly, and I point to my mistakes throughout the book. Districts like LAUSD are still trying to find student-proof ways to track, limit, filter, and control what students do on these devices, and with whom. Again, these digital walls, gates, and mandates occlude how we interact in the *real* world beyond schools, and I can hear an implicit *shame on you* echoing from educational forbearers such as John Dewey. At the risk of sounding like a broken record, if we are going to integrate mobile devices into classroom instruction (and I hesitantly think we should), we need to do so in ways that mirror what we hope students should be able to do once they graduate from our schools.

Running throughout the book is an argument about how the school environment destroys trust between adults and youth, and often destroys any active sense of agency on the part of learners. If a Genie gave you three wishes to transform the school environment, what would you change and why?

I'm going to start small and go loftier.

One year, as teachers were asked to sign off on a school grant proposal that we had little opportunity to provide actual input on, we discussed the limitations of throwing money and resources at bigger issues. LAUSD's failed iPad initiative is probably one of the clearest, recent examples of this. On the afternoon that we brainstormed what money *could* do, one teacher – Linda – proposed an idea that stays with me today. Simply put: fix PE. At SCHS, the PE classes – filled primarily with 9th- and 10th-graders (students statistically most likely to drop out of high school) – were overcrowded and under-supervised. For security purposes, students were locked each period within an area of dilapidated basketball courts and the school's gymnasiums, a chain link fence separating them from the rest of the school. It wasn't uncommon for PE teachers to have upwards of 80–100 students in each class, and for the locked gate of the PE area to act as a way for students to regularly skip other classes and remain hidden in the masses of students crowded in the area. With the same dollars that would be used for professional development interventions, purchasing SMARTboards, or other product- and service-oriented acquisitions, Linda pointed out that finding funding to, say, triple the number of PE teachers at the school could fundamentally transform the school's culture and outcomes. There are caveats, of course, to such dreaming. However, if ours is a Genie that could summon a handful of teachers in an area that is often overlooked, I could imagine it would make lasting cultural changes.

My second Genie wish is simple and based on work I've seen transform school culture. At the Schools for Community Action – a set of small state schools I co-founded and describe in the conclusion to *Good Reception* – a wall-to-wall support plan that implements a Restorative Justice approach to supporting student healing, classroom management, and community support is thriving. Though there are growing studies and support for Restorative Justice, its emphasis on acknowledging and healing wrongdoing is an approach that fundamentally shifts student, teacher, and administrative relationships at the school. It is *hard* work (and even I wonder about the capacities of a Genie!), but it is work that I would love to see more fully and authentically integrated right now. (As a brief note, I am wary of widespread district implementation of any program; as Restorative Justice grows in popularity, I wouldn't be surprised to see it watered down and shifting in meaning and value in different contexts.)

Finally – and acknowledging that this would have to be a powerful Genie(!) – I think it is necessary to spotlight and make visible the systemic issues of inequality that plague schools such as SCHS. There is no simple fix to racial, class-based, language-specific, or geographic forms of inequality that are inextricably linked to the power issues that affect contemporary understanding of academic achievement in US schools. There are, though, a *lot* of bad attempts at band-aid fixes for these issues. In just a couple of chapters of my book, for example, I point to poorly thought-through attempts by SCHS administration to address these topics through implementing school uniforms, new hall passes, changing bell schedules, and tardy-line policies. Without addressing the root causes of how schools for historically marginalized students are designed to fail, such surface-level approaches do little more than signal that well-meaning adults *tried*. If a Genie could center these inequities in the eyes of the public and in the policy-making decisions at local and national levels, I think we could (slowly) start making sounder decisions.

You have much to say about the different conceptions of time shaping the way teachers and students respond to mobile technologies at school. How do they differ and what factors have led to this gap in understanding? What are the implications of this gap for the ways we think about bringing mobile technologies into pedagogical practice?

I think how we understand the purpose of "school time" is one of the most out-of-sync aspects of public education in the US today. Simply put, students and teachers have different assumptions about what time means and how it is used in schools, during class time and during breaks such as passing periods and lunch. The traditional adult assumption (and one that I held for too long) is that – during class time – students should be solely working on class activities. Yes, these activities may include increasingly complex digital resources. However, these are still largely about specific kinds of practices and a relationship with technology that is oriented toward entirely academic purposes.

As bluntly as I can, I want to be clear: *this is not how adults function in today's workplace.* Even as I respond to these questions, my phone prods me for attention. I confess that I may have taken a peek or two at my Twitter feed and at my email inbox. Social relationships are pervasive and are not relegated to the time I punch the proverbial work clock.

Let's acknowledge that the few instances where adults do not regularly check-in with their phones while working are usually service-level jobs that barely provide a living wage for employees. In our practices in implementing these kinds of policies, there are two things that are alarming: we are training students to adhere to working-class kinds of employment practices, and we are stifling a culture that more fully reflects how other workplace environments function; school technology policies – as innocuous as they may seem – reinforce the historical, systemic inequalities that the Genie in the previous question just can't fix.

Let's also be clear that, at the heart of this decision around mobile use policies in schools, is *control.* The power of teachers is threatened by the disruptive practices of mobile technologies. Instead of moving toward new pedagogies, classroom orientations, and instructional practices, we have locked down how we treat classrooms and train teachers: we double-down on enforceable and punitive policies, rather than moving alongside of the rest of the changing world. All of this is a reminder that schools operate from an industrial, factory model. We have bells governing the end of one shift and the beginning of the next; we separate learning into discrete, disconnected units; and we structure the school physical and social space to silence voice and individuality. Technology policies only further entrench us in the *Learning to Labor* practices that Willis described more than 30 years ago.

Many of the youth pushed back at the idea that they might share contact with teachers through their normal social networking tools. Where does that resistance come from and how might teachers respect those views when designing activities that deploy social media at school?

As educators and researchers, we tend to talk about it as student resistance – we get to do that from an adult perspective of these issues of power in schools. For students, though, while their actions may indeed be resisting the desires and demands of authorities, these are issues of *trust.* Simply put, have teachers and school structures done enough relationship building, empathy support, and *listening* for students to choose to engage socially with teachers? Particularly in schools focused on high-stakes test results and district-wide expansion of charter schools that have the latest snake-oil-like pitch of a better path forward, the time for relationships – online or face-to-face – simply doesn't exist often enough.

Tied to issues of trust, we should probably also think about the meaning of mobile devices in schools today. We still tend to call them "phones," even though the vast majority of what we do on them isn't tied to this function and – as ex-Galaxie 500 member Damon Krukowski recently wrote in *The New Analog: Listening and Reconnecting in a Digital World* and discussed in a podcast[6] series – the sounds of talk and feelings of personalization have diminished in today's digital infrastructure.

I would encourage your readers to look at their own phone *right now*. What case is it in? What pictures are displayed on it? How do the apps on the main screen speak to your orientation in the world? These are personal devices that support personalized activities. In schools, they offer a portal to one of the few spaces closed off from the power and demands of adults. Asking students to sully such sacrosanct space is a big ask if we aren't willing to change the other structures in schools around these relationships.

In your own work, and that of you and the co-authors of *Participatory Culture in a Networked Era*, you have pointed to the fact that, on one hand these are personal devices and they often are leveraged in systems of "networked privacy." On the other hand, students use their devices to perform publicly for their peers aspects of their identity. From ringtones to cases to content loaded on screens, what is seen and heard via mobile devices reflects the identities of their users.

As a result of the issues of trust above, I've lately been encouraging teachers to start thinking about devices as ways to get to trust and engagement. I have teachers play Game of Phones[7] to highlight an easily adaptable, commercial example. The purpose isn't to use phone for accessing new, digital spaces or producing increasingly complex multimodal artifacts. Instead, these devices are for sharing identity, embracing multiple identities.

Many express concern that bringing mobile technologies into the classroom will result in greater distraction and that it is better to keep schools a media-free zone. How do you respond to those critiques?

In thinking about kids' attention being pulled from classes to their devices, the inner cynic in me wonders what kids are distracted *from*. We have come a long way from seeing schools as drab spaces of intense work. Wonder, imagination, and even fun are posed frequently in popular media as aspects of how good schools succeed. And so, when we talk about media devices distracting kids, we need to look critically at whether the materiality of schools is worthy to demand the attention of a generation of students that have many, many other ways to learn, interact, and socialize.

At the same time, there are elitist private schools that do embrace the media-free schooling utopias you suggest. Here, in the Silicon Valley, many of the wealthiest tech families send their children to schools that are "unplugged" from the media saturation that chimes for their children's attention. Such models mean we have to question whose children have the luxury of attending this type of school, and what kinds of home and after-school structures support these in-school practices. This points to the participation gap that you and your research team have written about.

Finally, as I mentioned earlier, we need to remember that we don't *live* in media-free zones. I increasingly believe that schools offer one of the places for students to actually learn authentic and real-world ways of utilizing their mobile devices in social environments. All of the multimodal composition stuff that kids do in classrooms is great, sure. However, just as valid, and more often denied, are the skills kids learn about how to deal with what is shared in online spaces (as explored in Carrie James's *Disconnected*), how to utilize digital tools for mobile forms of activism, and how to meaningfully integrate (or not) the lives we live in online environments into our day-to-day interactions. If not in schools, where do kids learn (and get meaningful support in) *how to be* on and with their mobile devices? Teachers and teacher educators are not being prepared for this shift in responsibility, and this has, increasingly, been a space of continuing research for me.

Your key case study in the book centers around the development of *Ask Anansi* as a classroom experience – in effect, an alternate reality game – which you felt dramatically increased some of your students' engagement with learning. Why? What factors led to its success?

The story of *Ask Anansi* starts a decade ago with how I found my way into the DML (Data Manipulation Language) community. Collaborating with now good friend and recent co-author Greg Niemeyer, we created an alternate reality game (ARG) for students in my class several years before *Ask Anansi*. That game, *The Black Cloud,*[8] proposed that the pollution in Los Angeles had grown sentient and was communicating with my first-period class via Twitter (then a very new platform). Through measuring air quality around their community, students took on new identities as storytellers and citizen scientists. Though we had an abundance of resources for this game (and the technology is currently being used to measure air quality via Google Street View cars), I was interested in how to replicate the possibilities of learning and identity that emerged in this game even with fewer resources.

With a different premise and different intended outcomes, I designed *Ask Anansi* as an ARG for my ninth-grade students (I share the design document and key principles in the game's DIY design in several appendices in *Good Reception*). This game, like much of the ARG design I have engaged in, speaks to how ARGs can lead to radical transformation. Greg and I write about this in the conclusion to our book, *Alternate Reality Games and the Cusp of Digital Gameplay.*

One of the key factors of success for an ARG like *Ask Anansi* is an intentional focus on the kinds of identities and feelings that the game is expected to foster. If students are exploring issues of inequality and *playing* with ideas of social transformation, those might be playful identities that porously move from within a game to outside of it; we push on the boundaries of what Johan Huzinga refers to as the "magic circle" that inscribes "play," in order to consider what identities and practices are taken outside of games and into the real world.

Often, teachers assume that games-based learning means digital games, but in this case, *Ask Anansi* was a game played in physical space but that led students to think more deeply about both the physical and digital worlds they inhabited. Can you say more about the underlying assumptions about technology that shaped this project?

The point of giving devices out to students and playing an ARG was never *about the technology*. Instead, by looking at points in school structures that could be adjusted, this was a study in how things like technology and play can transform the meaning, value, and opportunities of schooling. As the final chapters of the book highlight, the bigger outcomes of the study weren't simply about improving academics or doing fancy things on expensive devices.

Instead, *relationships* were what were most transformed during the time of this study. If we stop assuming technology will *fix* schools, its shortcomings in doing so won't seem so problematic. That is: just like we don't assume giving every student in school a set of pencils and paper makes them better learners, we shouldn't assume a Chromebook, iPad, or any other commercial product will do so either. Instead, we should recognize that pencils enable certain kinds of learning practices, as do mobile technologies. At the end of the day, leveraging these practices (and transforming schools) is going to be about transforming the relationships between students, teachers, and their broader community. *No technological advance is going to magically fix relationships, trust, or power in schools.* Once we can take this previous sentence for granted, we can probably make better collective decisions about instruction, school funding, and the structures of public education in the US and across the globe.

Many books on education stress success stories, but you are frank throughout about moments of failure or friction in your pedagogical practice. If you could relive your time in that school, what would you change?

I made a *lot* of mistakes throughout this study, and I try to detail them in the book in as much as I think that is useful for other researchers. I detail in my next answer a bit more about the technology-driven assumptions and mistakes I made. However, I actually think the thing I'd want to change is the scope of *Ask Anansi*. Often, when I talk with teachers about *The Black Cloud, Ask Anansi*, and other game-related activities I've done in my classroom, I hear both bewilderment and amusement at what transpired. Talking spiders, scavenger hunts, students out of the classroom running amuck: it feels like too much to try to accomplish and looks unanchored from standards-aligned classroom instruction. I have gotten both literal and proverbial pats on the head for this work: *this game is nice and all but I wouldn't be able to do this in my classroom and – even if I could – it wouldn't fit within my school's pacing plans.* And to that, I say "balderdash."

I wish I had worked with other teachers to implement an ARG like *Ask Anansi* across an entire department or grade level to highlight that this work isn't just possible but also is fun, intellectually engaging, and – in some cases – civically transformative. My recent work with teachers at a game-design school[9] has been pushing on how to sustain powerful and *gameful* approaches to learning and teaching.

You describe some of your students as being steadfast about not wanting to read, even though they possess core literacy skills. What

might these students teach us about the need to rethink what we mean by "reading" or "literacy" in the school context?

One of the most memorable exchanges for me during the study is an exchange I write about in which a student describes to his classmates how listening to an audiobook is "like reading."[10] This student, whom I call Solomon, highlights how small shifts in the consumption and production of texts push on the expectations of students and teachers alike. In this case, students are used to listening to audio via mobile devices passively – listening to music while talking with peers or engaged in other activities. By highlighting that audiobooks require the same kinds of active reading strategies as traditional forms of reading, Solomon helps illustrate that there's a little of the "old" in new and digital literacies today.

On the one hand, when we talk about literacies in schools and point to fancy devices such as tablets, netbooks, and laptops, we need to recognize that the vast majority of the work done on these devices is often replicating traditional forms of literacies: the Word document is a shinier version of a pad of paper, the Internet a more expansive version of the class encyclopedia, etc. That's not to say that things aren't different – there are affordances to writing on an Internet-enabled device that is capable of embedding GIFs and publishing for the entire world to consume. However, while I agree with the premise of this question – that such advances mean helping educators, parents, and students rethink what we mean by "literacy" – I also imagine a call for thinking more innovatively about what media production and reading *could* look like in schools.

I spend a lot of my time perusing (or fuming at) my Twitter feed. For better or worse, it is a persistent space that I look at and participate in. As a singular example, how would student writing, understanding of spatial geography, or statistical analysis *shift* if we accept the premise that civic participation today means students should have a grasp of how a tool like Twitter functions? As an English teacher, I've been fascinated with the idea of thinking about the messiness of interaction in hashtags like #BlackLivesMatter as an emerging and participatory form of *literature*. Again, Henry, your work, *Reading in a Participatory Culture*, has underscored my thinking here and points to new literacy shifts. As an additional pedagogical reminder within this example, discussions of, within, and around a platform like Twitter would also have to include an acknowledgment of how such tools are implicitly guiding participation within capitalist practices; a critical media literacy stance toward new reading and writing practices would require educators to also work alongside students to unpack how tools, from Twitter to classroom textbooks to the corporate devices students use in schools, are tied to neoliberal aspects of power and authority.

I offer this example of Twitter to highlight how instruction *could* shift to imagine what teaching for participation in a contemporary society could look like. Many friends and colleagues have been exploring what new digital practices mean in terms of student and teacher identities, and I recognize that these are huge opportunities for further reimagining literacy engagement and literature today.

Reflections

I write this just a bit more than a year after we first conducted this interview. In some ways, the beliefs and ideas I posed about teens, technology, and schooling are still largely the same. However, the contexts of the world in which young people are interacting, learning, and being assessed are in rapid flux. Further, the kinds of changes I've been thinking about here in the US do not have immediate, obvious solutions.

While schools continue to wrestle with how to properly utilize and support the digital needs of students within the twenty-first century, it is more apparent that the ecosystem of social media and persistent technology outside of schools is a perilously problematic one. Algorithms are sorting and filtering individuals in pernicious ways (Eubanks, 2017; Noble, 2018), media literacy has "backfired" (boyd, 2018) ushering in substantial distrust in the media, and young children have noted feelings of competing with their parents' mobile devices for attention (AVG Technologies, 2019). The role of technology in orienting young people to their civic world is one that has shaped adult practices and beliefs in ways that have been largely invisible. The current hand-wringing about foreign bots that helped seed discontent and mistrust within the US electoral system, and a rising moment of Trumpism that decries mainstream media as "fake news," only reinforce the complex contexts of how digital tools are implicitly teaching values and ascribing identities as consumers to our students.

To be clear, all of these issues were present as we engaged in our conversation and as I was writing *Good Reception*. However, the past two years in the US have pulled into sharp focus the intersecting roles of politics, technology, and civic identity in the lives of students and teachers. As I've argued recently (Garcia and Dutro, 2018; Garcia and Philip, 2018), the politics outside of schools fundamentally shape the conversations and feelings of students and teachers within schools. Fear about threats to a student's immigration status, suggesting legislation that writes groups of people "out of existence" (Green, Benner, and Pear, 2018), and a Supreme Court Justice nominating process that pushes against the #MeToo movement are all widely discussed issues that leverage digital tools to communicate and affect how students in schools *feel* each day. In this sense, the role of *empathy* as tied to technology and schooling has been the issue I've been most focused on since our conversation. If *Good Reception* illustrated that schools are ill equipped for the present reality of ubiquitous mobile technologies that upend traditional power structures, the current political context reflects a similar aloofness for addressing student feelings.

As I mentioned at the beginning of this reflection, there are no immediate solutions to the entangled mess of politics and technology that weighs heavily on the lives of young people in schools today. Schools continue to develop policies that restrict student agency, even as they run counter to how the rest of the world operates. Changes that support humanizing approaches to the full identities of students – in both digital and analog environments – will require a drastic realignment of how teachers are trained, supported, and compensated. This, too, is a current direction of my research since completing *Good Reception*.

References

AVG Technologies (2019). *Kids Are Competing with Mobile Phones for Parents' Attention*. [video] Available at: www.youtube.com/watch?v=QSr8QPaWiYg.

boyd, d. (2018). SXSW EDU keynote, *What Hath We Wrought?* [video] Available at: www.youtube.com/watch?v=0I7FVyQCjNg.

Eubanks, V. (2017). *Automating Inequality: How High-Tech Tools Profile, Police, and Punish the Poor.* New York: St. Martin's Press.

Garcia, A. and Dutro, E. (2018). Electing to heal: trauma, healing, and politics in classrooms. *English Education*, 50(4), pp. 375–83.

Garcia, A. and Philip, T. (2018). Smoldering in the darkness: contextualizing learning, technology, and politics under the weight of ongoing fear and nationalism. *Learning, Media and Technology*, 43(4), pp. 339–44.

Green, E., Benner, K., and Pear, R. (2018). *"Transgender" Could Be Defined Out of Existence Under Trump Administration.* [online] Nytimes.com. Available at: www.nytimes.com/2018/10/21/us/politics/transgender-trump-administration-sex-definition.html.

Noble, S. (2018). *Algorithms of Oppression: How Search Engines Reinforce Racism.* New York University Press.

PART III

PARTICIPATORY POLITICS

11

Introduction to Participatory Politics

In *Convergence Culture: Where Old and New Media Collide* (2006), I predicted that young people were acquiring skills, through their play with new media technologies and popular culture, that they would "soon" be applying to more "serious" purposes – among them, politics. As part of the MacArthur Foundation's research network on Youth and Participatory Politics, I spent the better part of the past decade studying and theorizing the new forms of politics that have emerged as young people have found their voices online and forged their own paths toward civic connection and political participation, often through their ability to remix, reframe, and recirculate resources they drew from popular culture. Many of those interviewed in this section are either members of the research network or people I met in the process of doing this research.

The Civic Paths research group at the University of Southern California conducted more than 100 interviews with young activists from a range of different social movements, trying to understand the routes which led them into more active engagement with politics, and the tactics they used to address the concerns of their generation. One of the things that kept surfacing in those exchanges was the idea that the civic needed to be rebuilt, that the language of mainstream politics did not address the concerns or awaken the imaginations of the emerging generation of citizens. In our book, *By Any Media Necessary: The New*

Youth Activism, we shared what we learned through our engagement with Invisible Children, the Harry Potter Alliance, the Nerdfighters, the Dreamers, American Muslim youth, and young libertarians, about their political lives. Through our work with other network members, we developed and elaborated on the concept of participatory politics as a way of describing the new identities and practices that have emerged.

Today, we are focused on the Civic Imagination, a concept that first surfaced through our conversation with youth activists but which we have expanded to reflect on civic life more generally. Across a range of different accounts of the role of the imagination in civic and political life, we have consolidated a model which stresses the role of the imagination in helping us to describe what a better world looks like, to understand ourselves as civic agents capable of changing the world, to map the process by which change might occur, to identify the shared interests of our community, to develop a sense of empathy and solidarity with others whose experiences differ from our own, and to imbue everyday spaces and practices with a sense of potentiality. We are interested in better understanding how groups such as #BlackLivesMatter or #NeverAgain have offered young people opportunities to actively participate in efforts toward social justice and, in the process, have encouraged them to bring their skills and imagination to the table.

My interest in the connections between imagination and politics was inspired to a large degree by my conversations with Stephen Duncombe (who was among the first people I interviewed when I launched my blog). When the interview below was conducted, his book *Dream: Re-Imagining Progressive Politics in the Age of Fantasy* had only recently been released. Barack Obama was just emerging as a presidential candidate for the Democratic Party, and we were both infatuated with the ways Obama was tapping into myths about the American past and hopes for its future, inspiring many youth to get involved in the political process for the first time. The Obama Campaign's emphatic "Yes We Can" chant, an English-language translation of a slogan previously associated with Cesar Chavez, carried the sense of empowerment and participation young people were seeking in their political leaders. Many of the campaign's practices tapped what Duncombe calls "ethical spectacle." Across this interview, he looked back to earlier American presidents (Franklin Delano Roosevelt, for example) and their use of media, as well as speculating on what a politics more fully engaged with popular culture might look like. As he notes in his reflections, some of these ideas carry even greater resonance today as we see the ways Donald Trump drew on his background in popular culture – as the host of a reality-television program, as a performer in professional wrestling, as the backer of beauty pageants, as a frequent guest on shock jock radio, as someone who uses Twitter to route around the news media, and as someone who helps to spread grassroots conspiracy theories. One can reasonably ask, as Duncombe does here, what a more progressive form of popular politics might look like, and what we can expect from the next generation of political leaders.

Any path forward for progressives in the Trump era is going to depend heavily on a coalition of women and people of color; their votes were central to the "blue wave," the successes that Democrats achieved in reclaiming control of the US House of Representatives during the 2018 election. Yet, as we talk about this more diverse and inclusive Democratic Party, there is still little talk about the role which Black youth might play in that process. Cathy J. Cohen was a fellow member of the Youth and Participatory Politics research network. She combines quantitative and qualitative methods to map the political lives of Black youth in her book *Democracy Remixed: Black Youth and the Future of American Politics*, which she discusses in the interview below. Her comments here took shape against the backdrop of the rise of the Tea Party movement in opposition to Obama's agenda, but she hints at the forces that would ultimately lead to Trump's rise to power. And the interview suggests the growing awareness of the impact of police violence and incarceration in ending the dreams of many Black youth for meaningful participation in their society. Responding to this shifting political context, Cohen has been in the trenches helping to identify and train the next generation of social movement leaders through the Black Youth Project, which she runs out of the University of Chicago. As the Project's website explains:

> The Black Youth Project will examine the attitudes, resources, and culture of the young, urban black millennial, exploring how these factors and others influence their decision-making, norms, and behavior in critical domains such as sex, health, and politics. Arguably more than any other subgroup of Americans, African American youth reflect the challenges of inclusion and empowerment in the post-civil rights period. At the core of this project will be an exploration of what young black Americans think about the political, cultural, and sexual choices and challenges confronting them and their peer group. We are especially interested in understanding what new factors help to shape or contribute to the social and political attitudes and behaviors of African American youth.

One path toward greater political participation and civic agency is to expand the range of stories we circulate within our culture, encouraging us to pay attention to and learn from other people's experiences, especially where they differ from our own. The work of Lina Srivastava – a media maker and social organizer – has helped to inform my own understanding of the role of storytelling in fostering political change. In the interview below, she describes what she means by transmedia activism, inspired in part by shifts in the way Hollywood tells its stories, but applied to addressing the concerns of some of the most oppressed and marginalized segments of society. She has done much of her work in India and other developing countries, calling attention to issues of poverty and sexual violence that impact the lives of many South Asian women. She describes here the ethical concerns surrounding western interventions in these debates, considering what questions we should ask before taking on responsibility for sharing other people's stories, and she describes the transmedia practices she deployed in some of the campaigns she helped to organize. Most of the interviews in this section focus on American politics during a period of abrupt transitions, so it seems especially important to test our understandings across a broader range of cultural contexts.

Much as Antero Garcia represented the next generation of educators who are applying the principles of participatory learning in his classroom teaching, Jonathan McIntosh represents the next generation of activists deploying new media platforms and practices to challenge the status quo. McIntosh sees remixing popular culture as esssential to speaking to millennials and postmillenials. His Pop Culture Detective videos, distributed via YouTube, engage with cult media in order to call out underlying stereotypes, especially those which fuel toxic masculinity, sexism, and homophobia. This project emerged from his work with Anita Sarkeesian whose own videos offering feminist critiques of video game tropes brought the unwelcomed attention of the alt-right and other trolls in what became known as #gamergate. Inspired by her example but seeking to address toxic masculinity as a male critic, McIntosh shares his own journey and his gender politics.

The book concludes with an extended interview with William Uricchio, who currently heads the Open Doc Lab at MIT. Uricchio and I were the co-directors of the MIT Comparative Media Studies Program for almost a decade. As a media historian, he takes the long view on media change, understanding our current moment of media in transition alongside other transformations in communication technologies. Here, he shares his perspective on the state of American journalism and documentary-making, calling attention to the ways innovators are deploying new media platforms and practices in reaching a more fragmented and dispersed public, in finding means of support when the traditional infrastructure has been disrupted, and in facilitating public discussions around contemporary issues that require complex and coordinated responses. As the website for Uricchio's lab explains:

> Open in its understanding of documentary's forms and potentials, the Lab is catalyst, partner and guide to the future of reality-based storytelling. The Lab understands Documentary as a project rather

than as a genre bound to a particular medium: documentary offers ways of exploring, representing, and critically engaging the world. It explores the potentials of emerging technologies and techniques to enhance the documentary project by including new voices, telling new stories and reaching new publics.

References

Cohen, C. J. (2010). *Democracy Remixed: Black Youth and the Future of American Politics*. Oxford University Press.

Duncombe, S. (2007). *Dream: Re-Imagining Progressive Politics in the Age of Fantasy*. New York: New Press.

Jenkins, H. (2006). *Convergence Culture: Where Old and New Media Collide*. New York University Press.

Jenkins, H., Shresthova, S., Gamber-Thompson, L., Kligler-Vilenchik, N., and Zimmerman, A. (2016). *By Any Media Necessary: The New Youth Activism*. New York University Press.

Further Reading

For more interviews dealing with participatory politics, see *Confessions of an Aca-Fan* at henryjenkins.org, with: Michael Counts (Jan. 31, 2007); Zephyr Rideout (Feb. 6, 2007); Peter Ludlow (Feb. 7, 2007); Wagner James Au (April 10, 2007); Sam Gregory (March 31, 2008); Ben Rigby (Sept. 1, 2008); Parmesh Shahani (Sept. 5, 2008); Jack Driscoll (Jan. 21, 2009); Dayna Cunningham (March 1, 2009); Jessica Clark (March 25, 2009); Andrew Slack (July 23, 2009); Eric Klininberg (Aug. 5, 2009); Harvard Web Ecology Project (Nov. 11, 2009); Marwan Kraidy (May 10, 2010); Nonny De La Pena (June 22, 2010); Joe Saltzman (June 28, 2010); Mary L. Gray (Sept. 10, 2010); Amber Day (May 3, 2011); Dan Gilmore (Sept. 13, 2011); John Palfrey (Oct. 13, 2011); Aniko Bodroghkozy (Sept. 24, 2012); Derrais Carter and Nicholas Yanes (Oct.

24, 2012); Matt Ratto and Megan Boler (May 23, 2014); Alison Trope (Nov. 24, 2014); Zizi Papacharissi (Jan. 19, 2015); Candis Callison (Feb. 9, 2015); Mr. Fish (Feb. 23, 2015); Ben Kirshner and Ellen Middaugh (May 24, 2015); Sasha Costanza-Chock (May 29, 2015); Danielle Allen (June 5, 2015); danah boyd and Mizuko Ito (Nov. 13, 2015); Tracy Van Slyke (Jan. 13, 2016); Black Hawk Hancock (May 25, 2016); D. C. Vito and Emily Long (Aug. 26, 2016); Dan Hassler-Forest (Sept. 1, 2016); Lori Kido Lopez (Sept. 15, 2016); Jose Antonio Vargas (Oct. 13, 2016) Eric Gordon and Paul Mihailidis (Nov. 1, 2016). Ramesh Srinivasan (April 10, 2017); Moritz Fink and Marilyn DeLaure (Oct. 30, 2017); Justin Reich (Jan. 16, 2018).

12

Manufacturing Dissent:
Stephen Duncombe (2007)

Stephen Duncombe is Professor of Media and Culture at New York University, and author and editor of six books on the intersection of culture and politics. Duncombe, a life-long political activist, is currently co-founder and co-Director of the Center for Artistic Activism, a research and training organization that helps activists create more like artists, and artists strategize more like activists.

Throughout the book *Dream: Re-Imagining Progressive Politics in An Age of Fantasy*, you embrace a politics based on spectacle. How do you define spectacle? What do you see as the defining characteristics of progressive spectacle, and how would it differ from more conservative forms of spectacle?

I guess I'd define spectacle as a dream performed, or, perhaps, a fantasy on display. Spectacle animates an abstraction and realizes what reality often times cannot represent. But I also like to use the term in a broader way: to describe a way of making an argument, not through appeals to reason and fact (though these certainly can, and should, be part of spectacle) but through stories and myth, imagination and fantasy. This definition covers what I call ethical spectacles, but also describes spectacles with fewer scruples: those engineered by the Nazis at Nuremberg, conjured up by creative directors on

Madison Avenue, or staged by Andrew Lloyd Webber on Broadway. So what separates my "ethical" spectacles from these? It's a complicated question and I spend about a third of my book exploring it, but if I had to sum up the core value of an ethical spectacle in one word it would be this: democracy.

Most spectacles are anti-democratic. They are about one-way communication flows and predictable responses. "They" engineer the look and feel and message of the spectacle, and "we" – the spectators – respond in a predetermined fashion. If this type of spectacle is successful, we give our consent or support: we march in lines and vote for the Party, or buy a certain brand of toothpaste. But it is always someone else's dream. Ethical spectacle follows a different formula. It's a spectacle where the lines between those who create and those who spectate are blurred – one which is dreamt up, executed, and acted upon by its participants. This makes for a sloppy sort of spectacle, one where spectators are also actors, where the mechanics of the staging are obvious to all involved, and where meanings and outcomes are not predetermined – but isn't this also the definition of democracy?

There's also another key difference between the spectacle I'm advocating for and that which we are used to experiencing: reality. Most spectacle is using fantasy as a replacement for reality. Think of President Bush's "Mission Accomplished" landing on the USS *Abraham Lincoln*. This was an attempt (imagineered by an ex-TV producer named Scott Sforza) to replace reality with fantasy: our president is a warrior prince, not a combat dodger; the war in Iraq is won, not just beginning. The approach I'm advocating for deals with reality differently, using spectacle to dramatize the real, not cover it over.

A great example of this is the Revd. Martin Luther King Jr.'s campaign to desegregate Birmingham, Alabama, in 1963. He went into Birmingham knowing the violent, racist reputation of the chief of police. In fact, he counted on it. And "Bull" Connor acted out his part: jailing school kids, turning fire hoses on picketers, letting dogs loose on peaceful protesters, and so on, creating those iconic images of the civil rights movement, and publicizing to a world media the reality of racism in the United States. I don't think it's a coincidence that the Civil Rights Act passed the next year. It's also no coincidence that the footage of Top Gun W couldn't be used by the Republicans a year after the staged landing – the deadly reality of the continuing war had leaked through the staged fantasy. As the presidential namesake of the aircraft carrier that Bush landed on once said: "You can't fool all of the people all of the time."

Ethical spectacle fools no one. It is at its best when it is obvious what it is: just a spectacle. Like the architecture of Las Vegas or the campy performance of pro wrestling, one can also stage spectacles that don't pretend to be reality but wear their constructed nature on their sleeve. They are spectacles which present themselves as spectacles. As such, these dreams performed become, in their own way, real. Illusion may be a necessary part of politics, but delusion need not be.

Your book poses some sharp criticisms of the kinds of political rhetoric which have emerged from "mainstream" perspectives within the Democratic Party. For example, you characterize progressive critics, such as Hillary Clinton or Joseph Lieberman, who embrace a "culture war" rhetoric, as playing into conservative stereotypes of "well-mannered, well-dressed, liberal elites," "busybodies," and "condescending experts" who want to use the power of government to enforce their tastes upon society. Why do you think Democratic leaders have been so quick to embrace a form of politics which is so strongly opposed to popular culture, and what do you see as the benefits of shifting the terms of the debate?

One of my friends, the activist David Solnit, once said: "all politics is theatre, just some of it is bad theatre." When it comes to popular culture, the Democrats seem clueless about their public image. Take Senator Hillary Clinton's press conference condemning *Grand Theft Auto*, for example. Here she was, before an international media, playing out the Right's stereotype of the Left: a bunch of superior-sounding, out-of-touch elites telling the rest of us what's good for us, and then using government regulation to make sure we can't decide for ourselves. Karl Rove couldn't have asked for anything better. (Nor could Rockstar Games, since that press conference likely sold bukoo copies of *GTA/SA* as people hurried out for a taste of forbidden fruit.)

Why the Dems are so clueless is a bit of a mystery. Part of it has to do with the history of liberalism in this country, which comes out of elite reform movements such as Prohibition (a once-progressive idea, along with eugenics!) as much as it arises out of labor and social movements (both of which are more interested in equality and justice than morality and culture). But this shying away from pop culture, I think, also has a lot to do with an abiding Enlightenment faith in the superiority of rationality and reason, and a deep suspicion of desire and fantasy – the very things, of course, which drive pop culture. This is a political problem since so much of politics is based in fantasy and desire, and Liberals these days are simply not very skilled in operating on this terrain. This split between rationality and fantasy is also a false one, these forces don't inhabit separate spheres, they coexist and intermingle in all of us. It's the old, and tired, mind/body split. It's time to move on.

You describe popular culture as a "ready-made laboratory" for studying the "dreams" of the American public. How do you respond to critics who might argue that you place too great a trust in market forces? You write, for example, "If culture stays, and sells, it means that it somehow resonates with the popular will. And anyone interested in democratic politics ignores such enthusiasm at his or her peril."

The biggest problem with ignoring popular culture, politically speaking, is not that you turn off this or that group of fans (the Dems could alienate every single NASCAR fan in the entire country and still sweep the elections), but that you ignore this powerful indicator of people's dreams and desires. As the great political commentator

Walter Lippmann once argued, politicians don't need to think much of popular culture, but they do need to think a lot about it.

I have a lot of problems living in a consumer capitalist culture, and my own cultural upbringing was in the decidedly anti-market world of punk rock, but even I recognize the value of appreciating popular culture in a society like ours. Unlike culture patronized by the aristocracy or funded by the state, commercial culture has to appeal to a wide enough audience to make it a profitable business. Yes, this appeal is not pure: marketing and star power can make any movie a hit the first weekend, but for that movie to still be selling the second and third, it had better resonate with the popular will. So if you want to figure out what ideas and aspirations are resonating with the public, a good place to start is with popular culture.

But, and this is a big but, the hit movie is not what we should be paying attention to – we need to dig deeper. What we really need to explore are the dreams at the root of the hit movie. That movie is only one manifestation of our desires, and a commercially acceptable one at that; we need to think of others. Take a hit movie like the original *Matrix*. As a fan, I can appreciate it as exciting entertainment, but as a politico, I'm interested in what it says about us as a people: our striving for personal power and to be part of a rebellious community, our desire to stick it to the man and reveal the truth (not to mention our love of cool toys and stylish outfits). Once you understand these forces, you can do other things with them. Pop culture is just one expression of our dreams. A progressive political system that empowers people, builds community, fights power, and reveals the truth – that might be another.

So far, we are seeing some signs of a more playful style of activism having an impact on the upcoming presidential election. Witness the spoof of the Apple 1984 campaign, "Obama Girl," or, for that matter, the video in which Hillary and Bill spoof the Sopranos. What do you think this YouTube-based politics might suggest about the potentials or limits of a politics which draws its images and language from popular culture?

I think you explore this far deeper, and far better, than I do, Henry, but it seems to me that accessible media production technology, the semiotic tool box we've all built from our life-long immersion in pop culture, and the new distribution apparatus like YouTube, have immense political potential. MoveOn.org demonstrated this in their "Bush in 30 Seconds" campaign. They asked their audience to make an anti-Bush advertisement – and received more than 1,500 of them, many of them better than anything a professional production house could create. This demonstrates the awesome power – and talent – of the "audience." This is, um, "poaching" at its best: political "fans" tapping into popular desire and, using pop-culture language, delivering a different message. At its worst, this pop culture poaching leads to the Hillary Clinton *Sopranos* ad.: using all the style of popular culture but ignoring the deep-seated reasons that such a series was popular. Clinton's approach is just using pop culture as a gimmick.

One of the things that interests me most about the explosion of media production is the multiplicity of messages and meanings that political campaigns have to contend with. This is not an entirely new phenomenon. Negative campaigning has existed since the beginning of American democracy (George Washington was accused of being the corrupter of a washerwoman's daughter), and the swiftboating of John Kerry was just a high-tech version. What is new this election cycle is the direct impact not of opposing professional campaigns, but of political fans. We've already seen how fans of Barack Obama have used pop-culture tropes to make him into a sex symbol and render Hillary Clinton as Big Sister. Political campaigns are just going to have to make peace with the fact that they cannot control their message, and that the message is going to be determined, in part, by their fans. This means that "unacceptable" material is going to be part of the political discussion and decision making.

We can either bemoan this fact – the debasement of the political process, and so on – or we can look for what might be more positive aspects. It could be argued that one of the things that are wrong with electoral politics today is that what is considered "acceptable" is determined by professional pundits, big media, and those who make large campaign contributions. Consequently, what is of interest to the majority of us is left out of the discussion. Certainly, Obama Girl isn't opening up a substantive political discussion of anything, but its very existence, and its popularity, suggest that we, the people, want something else – something more than the sanitized, pre-packaged, content-free politician packages we've gotten in the past.

There's no doubt that reducing serious politicians like Obama to a stud and Clinton to Big Sister debases politics, playing into old stereotypes about the sexuality of Black men and the controlling nature of professional women. But, as the means of mediated spectacle production and distribution continue to be democratized, I have faith that what will develop is a sort of bell curve of meaning. There will be offensive and malicious media spectacles as outliers on either side, but the critical mass of the center will open up substantive issues of political interest to the majority of citizens. Isn't this how democracy is supposed to work? This is merely democracy in the age of the mediated image.

You only briefly touch upon the rise of news comedy shows such as *The Daily Show* and *The Colbert Report*. Do you see such programs as a positive force in American democracy? How do you respond to those who feel that the blurring between news and politics trivializes the political process? What role does comedy play in the kinds of popular politics you are advocating?

I love *The Daily Show* and *The Colbert Report*. As someone on the Left, it is refreshing to see a progressive viewpoint expressed (even if only expressed ironically) in a way that makes me laugh and gives me pleasure. I also think that Stewart's and Colbert's use of humor can be deeply subversive: they use ridicule to show how ridiculous "serious politics" is, much in the same way that Jonathan Swift's "modest" proposal in 1729 made the "rational" case for solving the problem of the poor in Ireland by eating them. The political process is already a joke; these guys are merely recognizing it for what it is.

In doing this, they hold out the possibility of something else – that is, they create an opening for a discussion on what sort of a political process wouldn't be a joke. In doing this, they're setting the stage for a very democratic sort of dialog: one that asks questions rather than simply asserts the definitive truth. However, it's still unclear that ironic joking leads to the sort of popular response I'm hypothesizing above. It can, just as easily, lead into a resigned acceptance that all politics are just a joke and the best we can hope for is to get a good laugh out of it all. To paraphrase the philosopher Walter Benjamin: we can learn to find pleasure in our own destruction.

However, I think we need to take Stewart at his word: he's just an entertainer. It's really up to the rest of us to answer the questions he poses. Sometimes, I think we ask too much of culture: we expect it to solve our political problems for us. I don't think it can do this. It can create openings, give us insight, provide us with tools, but the rest is a political process that counts on all of us.

You contrast the ways in which FDR spoke to the American public with the ways that George W. Bush addresses us during his weekly radio-casts. What do you see as the primary differences? Most contemporary politicians who attempt to "explain" complex policy issues in the way FDR did get accused of being "wonks." What steps do you think could be taken to create a new political rhetoric which embraces the ideal of an informed public but doesn't come across as patronizing or pedantic?

The brilliance of FDR is that he and his New Deal administration, like King and his fellow organizers, recognized the necessity of spectacle in politics. Because of this, they worked hard to re-imagine spectacle in a way that could fit progressive, democratic ends. The 1920s were an era much like our own in its worship of celebrity: a mediated world of movie stars on the silver screen and sports heroes in the new photo-tabloids. But instead of merely condemning this state of affairs, New Deal artists and administrators re-imagined it, using photographs sponsored by the Farm Securities Agency and murals painted by artists of the Works Progress Administration to recognize and display a different sort of American: the dust-bowl farmer, the southern share cropper, the factory worker, the rootless migrant. By creating these counter-spectacles, they tried to turn the public gaze from stars to everyday (albeit romanticized) people, essentially redefining "The People" in the popular imagination. Make no mistake, this was a deeply political move, as valorizing everyday people was essential for garnering political support for New Deal political and economic programs.

Roosevelt's "fireside chats" also put the lie to the myth that spectacle has to run against reason. Over 30 times during his presidency, FDR addressed the American public on the radio. He would always begin these speeches with a warm "My friends." But what followed this simple greeting was a sophisticated explanation of the crises the country faced: the banking collapse, currency concerns, the judiciary, world war. This was propaganda. The speeches were scripted by playwrights who dramatized the case for the president's politics, and FDR spoke to people's fears and desires in a folksy, personalized language, but these fireside chats also took for granted that citizens could be reasoning beings with the ability to understand complex issues. In other words, FDR believed that rationality and emotion could exist side by side.

I wish contemporary politicians would learn from this. Instead, we get the "man of reason" like John Kerry, or the "man of fantasy" a.k.a. George W. Bush. Politicians need to understand – in a way that I think many producers of pop culture already do – that you can speak to reason and fantasy simultaneously. It's an Enlightenment myth that truth is self-evident: that all you need to do is lay out the facts of your argument and immediately people will acknowledge and embrace it. What FDR and King understood is that the truth needs help. It needs stories told about it, works of art made of it, it needs to use symbols and be embedded in myths that people find meaningful. It needs to be yelled from the mountaintops. The truth needs help, but helping it along doesn't mean abandoning it.

You discuss the public desire for recognition as the flip side of the relationship to celebrity culture. What lessons might progressives draw from reality television about this desire for recognition?

If there are two things that those on the Left love to hate (while secretly enjoying them), it's celebrity culture and reality TV. These play to our most base political desires: celebration of an ersatz aristocracy, and cut-throat competition; the driving fantasies of Feudalism and Capitalism, respectively. True, true. But it's a mistake to write them off as just that, for they also manifest another popular dream: the desire to be seen. What do stars have that we don't? Wealth and beauty, yes, but also something more important: they are recognized. What is reality TV about? The chance for someone like us to be recognized.

What sort of a politics can be based in a recognition that we desperately want to be recognized? First off, policies that make it easier to be seen and heard. Community TV, micro radio, free Internet access, net neutrality, and so on. If the populist Huey Long once called for a "chicken in every pot," in the mass-mediated age our slogan ought to be "every person an image." But it goes deeper than this, for the popular desire is not just about being seen as an image on a screen. This, in some ways, is just a metaphor for a far deeper desire: being recognized for who we are and what we are, our opinions and our talents – and this is the core of democracy.

The democracy we have today has little place for our opinions and talents. Our opinions show up as abstract polling data, and the only talents our political process asks for is our skill at forking over money to professional activists and campaigns, or our dexterity in pulling a voting lever. This professionalization of politics, whereby democracy becomes the business of lobbyists, fund raisers, and image consultants, has fundamentally alienated the citizenry from their own democracy. It's no wonder that we turn to culture to find these dreams of recognition expressed.

This issue really gets to the core of my *Dream*. My book is about learning from popular culture and constructing ethical spectacles, but the lessons that I hope are learned will lead further than making better advertisements or staging better protests for progressive political causes (though that wouldn't hurt). What I'm arguing for in my book is a reconfiguration of political thought, a sort of "dreampolitik" that recognizes that dreams and desires – ones that are currently manifested in pop culture – need to be an integral part of our democratic politics.

Reflections

Reading this interview after more than a decade, I am struck by how relevant some of these ideas still are – probably more relevant now than then. The US presidential campaign of 2016 made this patently clear. Enter Donald Trump, real-estate celebrity and reality-TV star, a non-politician who built his base by dreaming up nightmares of "bad hombres" streaming in over the borders, and transformed the election into a spectacle to end all spectacles.

In the debates, Trump failed at the most basic levels of logical reasoning. His "facts" were immediately refuted as lies, and his "arguments" consisted of a series of seemingly disconnected but emotionally charged words and phrases. After rolling over his hapless reality-based Republican rivals, Trump was left to face the Democratic contender, Hillary Clinton: competent, knowledgeable, and experienced; a self-described policy wonk who had a reasonable answer for every question posed to her. It was the perfect contest between the forces of fantasy and reality. Reality seemed the sure winner: the *New York Times* Upshot polls were predicting a 93 percent chance of Clinton victory only weeks before the election. Truth wins out!

So, what happened? While the experts and pundits who made sense of the election for us were assuming a game of politics-as-usual, Trump realized that a different set of rules were in operation. Trump's victory was due to many factors, of course, but his ability to thrive in a world whose contours have been shaped more by Las

Vegas fantasy (he is, after all, a casino owner) than Washington DC policy studies certainly helped him win his victory. There have been politicians who knew how to employ the tools and techniques of pop culture before, but by and large they've used these mass-cultural means to appear as stronger, friendlier, or more competent politicians than they, perhaps, actually are – taking Machiavelli's advice to rulers that it is important to appear virtuous, even if one is not, in reality. Trump is doing something different. He's not using tools of entertainment to appear a better politician, he is using politics as a better stage for his performance as an entertainer. It's nothing less than a paradigm shift.

So what is to be done? Nowadays, I work with social justice activists around the world, helping them to be more creative in their tactics and to learn from pop culture for their campaigns. In this work, I have been guided by a simple political premise, the first rule of guerrilla warfare: *know your terrain and use it to your advantage.* Whereas, once, this meant understanding physical landscapes of jungles and mountains, the political terrain of today is largely a cultural topography of signs and symbols, stories and spectacles. If we are going to fight – and win – we need to know how to navigate this new ground: not by retreating to a safe space where The Truth is known and Rationality and Reason always win the day, but by marching bravely forward into the fantasy lands where the real battles are being fought, guided by our dreams and armed with our imagination.

13

The Political Lives of Black Youth:
Cathy J. Cohen (2011)

Cathy J. Cohen is the David and Mary Winton Green Professor at the University of Chicago. She is the author of two books, *The Boundaries of Blackness: AIDS and the Breakdown of Black Politics* (1999) and *Democracy Remixed: Black Youth and the Future of American Politics* (2010). Cohen is also co-editor of the anthology *Women Transforming Politics: An Alternative Reader* (1997), with Kathleen Jones and Joan Tronto. Her articles have been published in numerous journals and edited volumes, including the *American Political Science Review*, *NOMOS*, *GLQ*, *Social Text*, and the *DuBois Review*. Cohen is the founder and Director of the Black Youth Project and the GenForward Survey Project. She has also helped to found a number of social justice organizations, such as Black AIDS Mobilization and Scholars for Social Justice.

Walk me through your title. What do you mean by "Democracy Remixed?" Why is this an appropriate metaphor for the book's findings?

I decided on the title of *Democracy Remixed* for a number of reasons. First, it seems to me that one of the interesting consequences of taking seriously the political ideas and actions of some of our most marginal citizens – Black youth – is that it pushes, challenges, and changes the nature of how democracy currently functions in the United States. If it doesn't, then something is seriously wrong.

For example, although there were historically high levels of Black youth voting in 2008, there are still serious challenges to the full participation of Black youth in our democracy. The issue of felony disenfranchisement and the general disproportionate impact of incarceration and policing in the lives of Black youth are made visible when we focus on their political lives. Far too many young Black people are unable to engage in the most basic of democratic practices – voting – because some states have taken away the franchise of those who have been convicted of a felony, even after they have served the terms of their sentence. Thus, if we are serious about facilitating the participation of young Black people in something as basic to democracy as voting, then we must examine and "remix" our ideas and laws about felony disenfranchisement.

Similarly, when we include Black youth as full and equal members of our political community, it means that we acknowledge their worth, and will debate and pursue politics that reflect their priorities and needs. For example, if young Black people were active participants in our policy debates, the political agenda might be "remixed" to include specific policies and programs such as quality education for marginalized youth, especially young Black people, who suffer from dropout rates of nearly 50 percent in some urban cities.

As a country, we might find ourselves designating more money to health programs accountable for erasing the disproportionate impact of HIV/AIDS, sexually transmitted infections, and mental health problems among Black youth. It might mean that we would do more to ensure that young people are not killed while playing outside their homes or on their way to or from school – a way of life for Black children in Chicago and other major cities.

The future of Black youth, as equal members of our political community, must be recognized to be the future of the nation. Their suffering is our suffering. And their progress is our progress. Only by remixing our democratic ideals and practices can we truly become an inclusive and fully functioning democratic community.

You begin your book with the story of your nephew Terry. How did his experiences inspire and inform the project? What would you like to see Terry and others of his generation take away from the ideas in your book?

... Terry, at least for me, represents many of the challenges of Black youth today. He has faced and dealt with many of the issues that confront the lives of far too many young Black people: violence, a failed educational system, incarceration, becoming a parent too early, and difficulty in finding a job – just to name a few. While these are familiar themes that have been outlined in a number of books on Black youth, what is different about Terry, and hopefully my arguments in this book, is that we both try to provide a more nuanced representation of Black youth than is regularly presented in other texts.

I believe that too often we publish monolithic representations of Black youth that focus exclusively on either their failure or their success. Bill Cosby is an example of one celebrity who has garnered a lot of media attention through the simplistic degradation of Black people and Black youth. I try in the book to detail the complex lives of Black youth. As thousands of young Black people who answered surveys, took part in in-depth interviews, and participated in focus groups for this book demonstrate, one has to pay attention to both the agency and structures that are a part of the story of Black youth.

When I talk with Terry about the difficulties he has encountered, his is a balanced account, noting structural barriers such as the lack of jobs one can find with a criminal record, but also detailing how he has contributed to his own struggles by, for example, having children without being able to fully care for them, emotionally and materially. While Terry is willing to discuss the impact of being tracked at an early age into special education classes, largely because the teachers in his school were unable or unwilling to deal with the learning challenges and energy of young Black boys and girls, he also is quick to point out that he did not take advantage of the educational opportunities presented to him. It is the complicated story of being young and Black in the United States today that I believe continues to deserve exploration in detail.

I hope the young people who read this book will first and foremost see themselves throughout it. One of the things that was really amazing about doing the research for this project was the willingness of young Black people to take time out of their schedules to talk to me and other researchers associated with the project. Repeatedly, they told us they were willing and eager to talk to us because people rarely asked them their opinions about the issues facing them and their ideas for solutions. So, I hope those same young people are able to hear their voices in the ideas and arguments of the book.

Second, I hope the book reminds both young Blacks and the nation as a whole of the centrality of young Black people to our democratic futures. Here I'm talking about not only the fact that Black youth suffer disproportionately from some of the most important issues facing the country – unemployment, the decline of public education, violence, HIV/AIDS – but also the fact that they are a central part of what is promising about the next generation. In 2008, Black and Latino youth came to the polls in record numbers to vote for the nation's first Black president. Their excitement, determination, and unprecedented turn-out signal the promise of an expanding democracy.

Third, and finally, I greatly respect young Black people for their political intellect, their determination, and their ability to honestly and openly state when they have made bad decisions. These young people are striving every day, like most of us, to do the right thing and be decent human beings. I hope this book affirms their efforts to work hard and do what is right, and their basic humanity.

I was very interested in the mix of quantitative and qualitative research methods shaping this study. What did each contribute to your understanding of the political lives of Black youth?

I wanted to use a mixed methodological approach to the book to reach a level of breadth and depth in reporting on the political lives of young Black people. Specifically, the research design started with a national representative sample of young people aged 15–25 that included oversamples of Black and Latino youth. By oversamples, I mean including larger numbers of Blacks and Latinos than might be necessary to make a traditional random sample, so that our statistical analysis of young Blacks and Latinos would be more reliable, and thus the margin of error would be smaller. In addition to ensuring that the sample would allow us to highlight and analyze the ideas and actions of Black youth in comparison to other racial and ethnic groups of young people, we also wanted to develop a survey that would focus on and be rooted in the lives of young Black people.

Many of the surveys used to explore the attitudes of young people start with White youth as the normative respondent. What I mean by that is that the survey is developed with a young White person in mind. We developed a survey that tried to tap into the lives of young Blacks. Toward that end, we did things like including questions on rap music and rap music videos, since we know that, as both a cultural and political form, hip hop – and specifically rap music – is central to the lives of Black youth. A lot of the statistical data included in the book come from two original data sets – the Black Youth Project, and another survey we mounted before and after the 2008 presidential election: the Mobilization and Change Project. All of the data from these projects are available to the public and can be downloaded through their websites.

Once we had the data from our new survey instrument in hand, we knew that these data would only allow us to say general things about the population of young people from different ethnic and racial groups. They would not provide us with the depth of knowledge needed to write a book that would capture and detail the nuanced political lives of Black youth. To gain greater knowledge and go deeper, we utilized two methods to gather additional qualitative data. One strategy we used was to carry out interviews with about 40 Black youth, most of whom had completed the national survey and lived in the Midwest. We targeted four cities – Chicago, Detroit, Milwaukee, and St. Louis – and conducted interviews with Black respondents in their city.

We were able to find respondents because, at the end of the survey, we included a question asking Black respondents if they would be willing to be interviewed in the future. Over 90 percent of Black youth answered affirmatively to the question, providing three contacts that we might be able to use to find them within a year. Even with this information, we were only able to find about 50 percent of the respondents who agreed to a future in-depth interview. After we confirmed the interview, graduate-student researchers drove to their town and sat down with each respondent for over an hour, assessing in a more free-flowing and detailed manner their thoughts on topics ranging from politics to the role of race in American society. Excerpts from these interviews are included as quotes throughout the book.

Finally, in 2005, and after the 2008 presidential election, we held a series of focus groups with young Black people in Chicago, aged 18–21. We used the early focus groups in 2005 to inform the development of our first national survey and our general work on the Black Youth Project. The focus group held in 2009 was used to get a sense of what young people thought about the election of President Obama and how they thought the policies of the nation's first African-American president would impact their lives. Again, I also use quotes from these focus groups throughout the book, especially in chapter 6.

You write, near the end of the book, "While the Obama Administration and other Black officials are attempting to avoid discussions of race, members of the Republican Party and the Far Right have escalated their racial and racist talks and attacks. These contrasting trends have meant that racial discourse is increasingly being shaped by, or at least framed by, the right wing." Clearly, you have in mind something like the Tea Party movement. How would you explain the expanding support that the Tea Party has received? What impact do you think such a movement has on the political lives of the Black youth you've studied?

I don't think it is a coincidence that recent polls show that only about 17 percent of Black youth support the Tea Party, compared to 34 percent of White youth and 15 percent of Latino youth. Black youth understand that the policies advanced by Tea Party candidates and members will mean a more limited role for the government in the lives of everyday Americans. And while many believe that the reach of the government has extended too far, Black youth realize that many of the opportunities secured by the mobilization of Blacks and others from the civil rights movement through the election of President Obama have only been implemented and protected by an active and expanded federal government.

Thus, a significant part of the Tea Party agenda – that which would repeal recently won health reform or pursue deficit reduction by slashing needed safety-net programs, or reduce funding for public education, or generally decrease and constrain the work of the government – would detrimentally impact the lives of Black youth, especially those who are most vulnerable.

Beyond the specific policies of the Tea Party, I believe that their exaggerated discourse, especially as it targets President Obama, attacks his policies, and engages in racial baiting, will reinforce the idea held among Black youth that racism remains a major issue in this country and that Black people are treated as second-class citizens in the political community. These young people have watched as the Tea Party held rallies in which President Obama was demeaned and depicted as other, an unspeakable evil on a par with Adolf Hitler. They believe that, while some of the objections to President Obama are based on the political agenda he has pursued, other motivations for the challenge to President Obama have everything to do with the fact that he is Black.

In response to such actions on the part of some members of the Tea Party, it seems that President Obama and his team have made a decision to try and stay above the fray of racial politics, adopting or letting stand a color-blind approach to race in the United States. My concern, as you quote in the question, is that the absence of leadership by President Obama on the topic of race and racism has allowed the right wing and some more extreme Tea Party types to step into the gap and promote their decidedly pre-civil rights movement view of the ideal racial order.

In contrast to the continued activity of the right on questions of race and racism, those public officials who might traditionally be mobilized to fight for and articulate a political agenda meant to improve the opportunities and lives of Black youth – specifically Black and progressive politicians such as Barack Obama – are exceedingly reticent to make and defend an explicitly racialized agenda. And so Black youth are left to fend for themselves on issues of race and racism, again learning the lesson that politicians are not to be trusted and that, even in an environment where expansion of our political community is promised, some will fight the equal rights and inclusion of Black youth seemingly forever!

As you've noted, the perspectives of Black youth are rarely discussed as part of our understanding of contemporary politics. What do we understand differently about the current political scene if their views are factored into our analysis?

I think it is hard to understand and think effectively about the issues that confront us without thinking about the perspective and lived experience of Black youth. As I discussed in a different question, Black youth are at the center of many of the most troubling issues confronting the country. Issues ranging from the decline in public education to the rise in incarceration and the dominance of the prison industrial complex all disproportionately impact Black youth. So it will be hard to develop effective and inclusive policies, programs, and approaches to these issues without seriously considering the perspectives, and including the insights, of Black youth.

However, it is more than just a simple gesture of inclusion that is needed when thinking about how Black youth help us to understand and imagine the political scene differently. We have to acknowledge that young Black people often have a different take on issues from other groups of young people, a take that necessitates different policy choices and political collaborations. For example, if we look at the issue of whether we are currently – or are even approaching – a post-racial state, Black and White youth think very differently about this issue.

Since the election of Barack Obama, much has been made of the generational divide in the populace. Some have suggested that, once the so-called millennials come to dominate the political domain, many of the thorny social issues that have caused great debate and consternation among the American public will be resolved. This line of reasoning implies that young people who embrace and personify a more inclusive society will eventually take over policy-making and thought leadership, moving both areas in a more liberal direction. Commentators point to the significant differences in opinion regis-tered among various generations on topics such as same-sex marriage and abortion as evidence of the more inclusive worldview held by the majority of young people.

The promised harmony around social issues that is presumably evident among younger Americans extends beyond the confines of sexually infused social policy to the prominent and always simmering issue of race. An article published in the *New York Times* suggests that much of the problem of race and racism found in the Tea Party and the NAACP has to do with the fact that they both are largely comprised of older members who grew up as the targets or beneficiaries of Jim Crow. Columnist Matt Bai writes, "The Tea Party and the N.A.A.C.P. represent disproportionately older memberships. And herein lies a problem with so much of our discussion about race and politics in the Obama era: we tend not to recognize the generational divide that underlies it."

As evidence of this substantial generational divide, Bai cites pre-midterm data from the Pew Research Center indicating that "there is nearly a 20 point spread between Mr. Obama's approval ratings among voters younger than 30 and those older than 65." Perhaps Bai's most important observation is one that he seems to add almost as a throwaway: his comment that "These numbers probably do reflect some profound racial differences among the generations." I show in the book that significant and profound differences in how young Whites, Blacks, and Latinos think about such topics as racism, citizenship, and gay and lesbian issues still exist today, and that these differences are a defining feature of American politics as practiced by the young, even in the age of Obama.

Far from the generation of millennials signaling the end of race or even the beginning of a post-racial society, I present data in the book that suggest that deep divides still exist among young people, with Black youth particularly skeptical about the idea of a post-racial anything. I note in the book that, in a survey we administered seven months after the 2008 election, we asked 18- to 35-year-old respondents whether they believed racism was still a major problem. The divide between Black and White young people was stark: 68% of Black youth stated that racism remains a major problem, compared to 33% of White respondents and 58% of Latino respondents

A similar split was evident when we asked whether Blacks had achieved racial equality. A near-majority of Whites (48%) thought Blacks had achieved equality, compared to 15% of Blacks and 39% of Latinos. As we know, the racial landscape is far more expansive than one that accounts for just Blacks and Whites. When asked whether Latinos had achieved racial equality, support for this assertion dropped among Whites. In fact, only 29% of Whites, 16% of Blacks, and 20% of Latinos believed that Latinos had achieved racial equality.

In the many articles written about the generational shift in attitudes on social issues, such as gay marriage or even race, few, if any, take the time to disaggregate the data by race and ethnicity to determine whether there might be divergent trends among the many groups comprising "youth." When researchers disaggregate their data (that is, if they have sampled enough people of color to pursue statistical analysis of different racial and ethnic groups), they often find that there are significant differences in how young people from the various racial and ethnic groups that make up the American populace think about not only same-sex marriage and abortion, but also race. If leaders continue to make policy, and academics insist on writing articles, with data assuming that the ideas of White youth represent the attitudes of all young people, they are all in for a rude awakening.

As the demographics of the country continue to move from one dominated – in population and power – by Whites to one increasingly populated by individuals of color, our analyses must start paying attention to the ideas, attitudes, and actions of young people of color. Making the experiences of Black and Latino youth central to our understanding and "work" around race provides a very different perspective in terms of what we must do. In the realm of race, the experience of Black youth – and, at times, Latino youth – is that race still figures prominently in their lives, shaping where they can live, whether and where they work, and how state authorities, such as the police, treat them. For these young people, racism still blocks their access to full citizenship, in particular the psychological aspects of believing that one belongs to and is valued in the larger political community. In the book, I use the experiences of Black youth to underscore the necessity of not just including, but highlighting, the voices and experiences of Black youth if we are to bolster democratic practice in the twenty-first century.

Reflections

While I am sure there is always tremendous change over any ten-year period, it is hard to imagine that more could have changed and stayed the same in the ten years since Henry and I first talked about the release of my book *Democracy Remixed: Black Youth and the Future of American Democracy*. For example, I could never have imagined that, between 2008 and 2018, we would elect the country's first African-American president followed by a president who traffics in White supremacy, using racism to divide and conquer the electorate.

Actually, it is the similarities between the events that surrounded the launch of *Democracy Remixed* and what is happening today that should alarm us. The opening pages of *Democracy Remixed* recount the murder of Derrion Albert. Derrion was a 16-year-old Black honor-roll student in Chicago, Illinois, who was beaten to death on his way home from school on September 24, 2009. We know the specifics of Derrion's brutal murder because it was caught on footage from a cell phone – a video that was seen around the world as it was both shown by broadcast media and posted on Internet sites such as YouTube. As can be seen on the video, Derrion was hit repeatedly with a board and then stomped while on the ground by a group of boys and young men. He was pronounced dead on the same day of the attack. Sadly, nearly a decade after the killing of Derrion Albert, many in the country are still consumed with and consuming images of the killing of young Black people. From Trayvon Martin to Michael Brown to Tamir Rice to Rekia Boyd to Sandra Bland to Laquan McDonald to Korryn Gaines, we are reminded daily of the precarious status of young Black people. They exist in the world as queer subjects, the targets of racial normalizing projects intent on pathologizing them across the dimensions of race, class, gender, and sexuality, making them into deviants while normalizing their degradation and marginalization until it becomes what we expect – the norm; until it becomes something that we no longer pay attention to.

What is different today is that this onslaught of Black public death at the hands of police officers and vigilantes has ignited protests across the county. Daily, young people are refusing to be silent, as the humanity of Black people and, more broadly, those on the margins is demeaned. And, far from being an updated version of the civil rights movement, the organizations that comprise the Movement for Black Lives are leading a transformative moment in Black politics, where centers of resistance range from Ferguson to Cleveland to

Baltimore to Chicago, and are fueled by rage at the violence directed at Black people. This new iteration of the Black radical tradition is guided by a Black queer feminist politics that centers an intersectional approach to organizing, highlighting the many identities that Black communities and Black bodies encompass, but with a focus on those most marginal: Black women – cis and trans; Black poor people; Black gender non-conforming folk; and Black gay, lesbian, and queer people.

While I think back to the many topics that Henry and I discussed almost ten years ago, there is a clear theme that has stood the test of time, namely that "As equal members of our political community, the future of Black youth must be recognized to be the future of the nation. Their suffering is our suffering. And their progress is our progress. Only by remixing our democratic ideals and practices can we truly become an inclusive and fully functioning democratic community."

14

Transmedia Activism: Lina Srivastava (2016)

Lina Srivastava is founder of CIEL | Creative Impact and Experience Lab. The former Executive Director of Kids with Cameras, Lina has worked with organizations including UNICEF, UNESCO, the World Bank, and FilmAid – with award-winning documentaries including *Born into Brothels*, *Inocente*, and *Who Is Dayani Cristal?* – and on media projects including *Priya's Shakti* and *My City Istanbul*. She is on faculty with the School of Visual Arts' Design for Social Innovation, a Fulbright Specialist candidate, on the US State Department's American Film Showcase roster, a Rockwood Institute / JustFilms fellow, recipient of a Rockefeller Foundation leadership grant, a Boehm Media fellow, a fellow of the Royal Society of Arts, and a graduate of New York University School of Law.

The term "transmedia" is one which has become increasingly expansive, meaning somewhat different things to different thinkers. Through your work, you've talked about transmedia activism. How do you define that concept? Why do you think transmedia is especially valuable as a model for thinking about activism and mobilization?

It's the combined core of story, community, and collaboration that I seized on the first time I heard and understood the term "transmedia."

As I thought about the methodology of creating and distributing stories through this framework, I realized the potential for effective social action that emanated from co-creating stories through multiple perspectives that illuminate social, political, and cultural contexts.

I've been working in social impact for 15 years. The work I do centers primarily with nonprofits and institutions that focus on human rights and international development, or with individual artists and filmmakers who create socially relevant art. Through this intersection, I've found that at the very foundation of social change are stories.

And while it appears to me we've hit peak noise on discussions of the role of storytelling in social impact, creative expression and culture are still, in my opinion, very underutilized in the social impact fields. We rely heavily on data and policy frameworks, and when we do bring in story, it is still more often to communicate the impact of a program than it is for using it as a strategic driver of change.

You need narrative to spur social action that resonates with and is relevant to communities that are fighting for positive change. You need to know what's happening at the blood-and-guts-and-feelings level for people – and you need to know what the possibilities and costs of our policies and actions are to actual human beings.

Otherwise, what are we fighting for?

So, storytelling – and transmedia in particular – lets me, as a storyteller and a social change agent, illuminate the human side of things.

Activism and mobilization, two distinct ways of effecting social change, at their core rely on community, participation, and collaboration. There's more to activism or social impact work than these things, of course, but these are essential – and when they are absent, we often get top-down, simplistic, and paternalistic interventions that are ultimately unsustainable because they don't emerge from perspectives that are based in local contexts.

Beyond that, transmedia has the advantage of allowing for people to travel among multiple entry points, and for immersion, both of which are key in allowing for multiple narratives and for complexity.

And transmedia answers the question: "How do you tell the story of a system?" There's a danger in social change when you tell a story from one perspective, or from one node in the system. For example, when one thinks about, say, water issues, you may have to think about infrastructure, climate change, safety and security for those getting the water, privatization vs. public access, or sanitation and health, etc. You may work only on one of these aspects, but you have to understand how one issue affects the rest and how one shift in the system can change things throughout the system. And you have to know how to tell that story.

True social change comes when solutions are systemic, and transmedia itself – however we define it – has been a social innovation that allows us to view our ecosystem of issues and create stakeholder engagement around systemic change. And one that allows us to get into the heart and soul of how these issues affect people and their lives.

So I coined the phrase "transmedia activism" in 2009 to describe this process: the coordinated co-creation of narrative and cultural expression by several constituencies who distribute that narrative in various forms through multiple platforms, the result of which is to build an ecosystem of content and networks that engage in community-centered social activity.

Another way of saying this is that we use story to effect social change by engaging multiple stakeholders on multiple platforms to collaborate toward appropriate, community-led social action. (And I note: the phrase may specify "activism," but the framework is meant to be used for various types of social impact or mission-driven work.)

I should have been broader when I thought of the term, but this one sounded better than, say, "transmedia impact," and I acknowledge its linguistic limitations. And I also will acknowledge here that I don't always use the term "transmedia" at all when describing my work, as sometimes it's more appropriate to use alternative terms that will be more easily understood.

When we build a story universe for social change under this framework, we think first in terms of an ecosystem of issues, social and cultural conditions, communities, and solutions – and not only about the narrative arc of the story.

I'm not sure whether my definition works for other thinkers or not. I've rarely been one to indulge in discussions around the definition of transmedia, because to me the debate was always a distraction from what I thought to be the core utility of the term, which was to map out a new method of exploring the ways communities were already working together and the ways they were already using culture to effect social change.

At the time that I was working on the "transmedia activism" framework, about eight years into my work in social impact, discussions around multi-platform narrative as a strategic tool were still fairly nascent in the social impact world, but storytelling per se is not an original concept in social impact.

People had talked about storytelling for years, and the success of story- and culture-based feedback loops was well documented. So I wasn't establishing anything new. I was putting a frame around narrative in a way that plugged into numerous emerging discussions, including social innovation, human-centered design, and digital media, and packaged those discussions under one frame.

As I read your writing, your concept emphasizes multiple contributing authors working with shared assets, as opposed, say, to a single author working across media. Why do you find this idea of collaborative authorship important for thinking about social action campaigns?

Collaborative authorship opens up possibilities, as I discussed above, for multiple perspectives, which is crucial to social action that is grounded in both local context and in larger political or cultural trends. On the creative or artistic side of transmedia, we hear a great deal about the dissolving of boundaries between artist and audience, or creators and fans. The analogy for social impact is not one of the taking down of boundaries between various communities and stakeholders.

If we accept that story and media are powerful tools to influence the way people understand issues (*knowledge*), experience the issues (*engagement*), see themselves and others in relation to the issues (*perception*), and what they do to cause these issues to shift (*action*), then we can see that NGOs (non-governmental organizations) and activists who commit to a process through which their various stakeholder communities and influencers take shared ownership of their mission-related story and media, build an advantage of shared support for their goals, activities, and outcomes.

By identifying the narrative underlying the full spectrum of engagement to action, and then by collectivizing ownership of that narrative, transmedia bears the potential to break down the unidirectional construct – "us" helping "them" – that is often at the heart of many traditional aid and international development efforts, instead creating a network of change agents that use narrative as a tool to work toward shared goals, activities, and outcomes.

This has the added benefit of having the potential to shake up existing power structures and to move away from paternalistic, patriarchal narrative and design. Transmedia strategies, in allowing diverse and multiple authorship, have the potential to create better streams of participation for community-centered design or "local voice" – i.e., voices coming from an affected community, to tell its own stories and participate in or lead solutions-building ...

You have been especially concerned about "the ethics of telling other people's stories." What do you see as some of the most common ethical failures that occur when human rights advocates attempt to mobilize around stories from the field, stories that deal with the real-life struggles of real people? What kinds of ethical frames should such campaigns adopt to make sure they are being fair to those people whose life stories are entrusted to them? How can filmmakers and activists avoid making "poverty porn?"

We have to stop treating other people's stories as if they are ours for the taking and shaping. We have to recognize that agency and self-representation are crucial to social change, and people's perspectives of their own situations matter. As Darren Walker recently said in a discussion at the Ford Foundation, cultural narratives drive why inequality and exclusion persist.

We may believe that our colonial period is behind us, but neocolonialist perceptions persist in our institutions and in our cultural narratives. Media outlets trade in savior complex stories to audiences who consume simplified narratives that allow them to feel good and ignore structural inequities, a relationship which leads to an ecosystem of cultural narrative that continually misrepresents poor, marginalized, and at-risk communities. And it's very easy to fall back into these tropes.

A few years ago, I wrote a post criticizing the phrase "giving voice to the voiceless." It's a phrase I dislike quite a bit, and while I hear it a bit less these days, it still manages to encapsulate the way we sometimes perceive other people we are seeking to "help," especially if they are poor, or seen as poor (e.g., the way we in the west still see most of Africa). I said:

> If we seek to truly collaborate with people ... to advance positive social change, we need to shift our thinking about who contributes to the "project." It's much more helpful to think of each other as equal partners who bring to the table various assets ... For example, one partner might bring access and resources, while the other one brings local learning, stories and knowledge [cultural assets]. I'm not naive enough to believe that in our current system ... there isn't a power advantage in being the one in control of the financial resources and of the avenues that distribute information. But we have to learn and teach a different perspective on what is contribution, what are valuable assets and resources, and who plays what position on the team? ... [C]alling people "voiceless" discredits their ability to contribute. All of us need to recognize participation and contributed assets as valuable tools ... as leverage to effect positive change.

As artists and storytellers, we have an ethical responsibility to understand that we cannot impose "voice." I will acknowledge that there is power in engaging audiences through language that we know, through tropes we are used to, through allowing us to feel good about the work we do – and, when done well, it can contribute to both effective change and good storytelling.

But, as change agents, we are not speaking for someone else. We are primarily serving one of two functions in relation to people in an affected community: either acting as their proxy, or working in collaboration with them. We might be providing access to avenues that disseminate their voice, and that's our role in the project, but we have to interrogate how our position may be affected by privilege or top-down perspectives.

As artists, it is our obligation to open up new frames of reference. In the realm of transmedia, each piece of work related to an issue can transform audiences' frames of reference, and it's our role – and within our reach – to use story to put pressure on existing frames that dehumanize subjects, and to shift the angles to expose humanity in the form of lived experience and cultural context....

Many of your projects are connected with documentary productions, whereas often transmedia is understood in relation to fictional storytelling. What added value comes from expanding the scope of documentary productions through transmedia?

There is value in increasing the surface area through which you can engage stakeholders and partners on issues, which you can do by creating multiple entry and participation points through transmedia. In my mind, when I start thinking through strategy, I see the expansion of the core story almost like a taffy pull – you can expand the scope of your story to encompass both the multiple perspectives I mentioned above and also the ways in which stakeholders can take effective action that proceeds from the story....

On a related note, I work with nonfiction content more so than fictional because, in the realm of social impact, truth is often far more resonant than fiction. Or, looking at it another way, who needs fiction when truth is strange enough?

I will say that I am wary of pop fiction that is spectacle and gesture and political theatre simply for the sake of itself. I do think, however, that fictional content is underused in social impact and that there is much more scope for transmedia producers and artists to experiment with strategic audience engagement and impact.

Tell us more about *Priya's Shakti* as an example of how fictional storytelling can also be used for social change. What motivated this project? What did you hope to achieve? Why did comics turn out to be an effective resource around which to base such a campaign?

Priya's Shakti is one of the few fictional projects I've worked on and it was simultaneously challenging and fun. (Well, as much as you can have fun with the issue of gender-based violence [GBV].) The motivation of this project was the 2012 bus rape in New Delhi, India, and the aftermath protests, which amplified and intensified decades of activism in India around women's rights. It was a seminal moment for the country to come together around the issue of gender-based violence.

The project's creator, Ram Devineni, was there to participate, and he came back with the idea of doing a project that would start exploring cultural patriarchal tropes through popular culture and new media that would engage youth. Graphic comics with embedded augmented reality (AR) turned out to be a unique and engaging method for youth to come to the material.

More importantly, we were able to embed real stories of rape survivors within the AR components, aimed at increasing the reach of our nonprofit partner Apne Aap into new audiences. And it set the stage for a series of workshops held with disadvantaged school-aged children to let them create their own comics.

In an essay for the *Huffington Post*, you describe the ways you want to challenge some of the stereotypes surrounding the representation

of women's issues in India via mainstream and global media. In what ways do Priya and her story challenge such stereotypes?

It was very important to me, as a feminist and a person of Indian origin, to not have the project be a part of the narrative that "India has a rape problem." While not attempting to whitewash what was happening on a societal level, I was unsettled by the narrative – because it misrepresented Indian society, but also because it pushed aside the reality that GBV is a global problem. And, by and large, Indian feminists were deeply offended by the manipulative and unbalanced representations in western press and in projects such as the BBC film *India's Daughter.*[11]

The rape and protests afterward were a defining moment for Indians and Indian feminists, marking a point in time for all their decades of struggle and really good work. It was important to me to honor and support the work that activists and development professionals were already doing in India, while still presenting an engaging story appropriate for young people – and, more importantly, to tie the story to grassroots and community-driven action in the face of a waterfall of international attention. It was a difficult balancing act, and one I'm still evaluating.

There are, of course, limitations to using a comic book as a vehicle. It's a simple narrative, aimed at a young demographic. In our case, the book was also centered in Hindu goddess mythology, which was risky on a number of levels. But it was also imagery that we, the creative team (most of whom were of Indian origin or sensitive to Indian culture), had all seen throughout our lives and that was instantly recognizable – and that we thought we might be able to subvert into a story of self-determination.

And I think, ultimately, Priya is a subversive character. She is framed as an everywoman who reaches beyond her tragedy and circumstance by tapping into her own sources of power to reframe herself as a leader on her own terms, and one who challenges existing norms through art and love. She is an everywoman who becomes a superhero of a sort.

And if she's a superhero, her super-strengths to fight the patriarchy are song, nonviolence, and compassion.

In some ways, Priya's story merges together the mythological tradition in Indian popular culture and the superhero genre. Why did these seem to be particularly effective building blocks for this project? I am struck by the parallels with and differences from the *Burka Avenger* Project in Pakistan, which also uses the superhero genre to speak to the rights of women – in this case, the rights of Islamic women to education.

South Asian societies, rich and wonderful though they are, do still carry patriarchal challenges to female self-empowerment and self-direction. While I would argue that Priya isn't a traditional superhero, while the Burka Avenger is (and she's a fantastic character in a great storyworld), the superhero genre is both an innovative and a safe space in which to explore and advance strong, empowered, independent females as role models for young girls.

When we spoke, you said you were turning your attention more and more toward building up the creative sector, so that projects may have greater sustainability. What do you see as some of the most urgent needs in terms of helping to provide voice to media creators around the world?

As I wrote above, there needs to be more attention paid to business models and financing of these projects, and I'm very excited that I've started exploring ways to make the creative impact sector more vibrant and sustainable. I'm building out a strategy for how to do that through my company in partnership with social enterprise experts. And while I'm not intending to become an investor, I'm excited to say I've just made my first angel investment in a creative social enterprise in Haiti.

There also needs to be more training and project incubation opportunities for creatives in lower- and middle-income communities and regions, which requires donor and investor education. Similarly, another need is to actively develop audiences for these projects. This requires a critical infrastructure, more robust distribution opportunities, and frankly more trust on the part of distributors that people will come to see or interact with this content (even if it is perceived to be "foreign").

Finally, as I've said in various ways above, we need to let go of some of the control over who tells whose stories, and let creators tell the stories of their own communities – and be there to partner with them, and explore their experiences.

Reflections

Reading my interview now throws into stark relief just how much the world has changed – and how much my work has shifted in response.

When we did the interview, Brexit and Trump hadn't yet happened. The concerted erosion of democratic norms and international cooperation, the rise of nationalism and xenophobia, the wicked problems of forced displacement, inequality, and climate change were largely talked about only at the margins of mainstream discourse. My interview reflects discussions in the innovation, design, and media sectors on how we could use our skills for social impact. While working with affected communities as an advocate in human rights and international development made me skeptical of some of the sectors' more paternalistic theories – for example, that emerging media such as VR could function as "empathy machines," or that any single documentary project would lead to social change – I did share the hope that artistic practice and storytelling that pushed boundaries could set the stage for positive impact. I'm not sure that's entirely true for me at the moment.

What felt like hope in 2016 feels like complacency now. I want to get back to that hope and to the joy of artistic practice, and soon, but in our current political moment I am feeling a sense of urgency I didn't three years ago.

None of the projects I've worked on since 2016 uses video, let alone immersive media. At the time of this interview, I was working on *Priya's Shakti*, a project using AR, and *Traveling While Black*, using VR. I have since stopped working on both, and on other projects like these. I still believe there is a role for these kinds of projects in the fight for social justice if they connect effectively to social movements – but there isn't a role for me that I want to occupy, at least not right now, because I am more concerned with social practice than I am with artistic output.

Since the interview, then, my work has gone as close to "analog" as you can go in a digital world. I have been focusing on direct dialog, messaging and storytelling to counter xenophobic narrative, and analyzing the kinds of processes and relationships needed to catalyze transformational change.

In practice, this means researching and drafting white papers, such as one co-written with the US and Kenya-based organization FilmAid on the efficacy of media interventions for the Syrian refugee crisis; and building toolkits, such as one on creating a welcoming culture for migrants (supported by CAMMINA and Hispanics in Philanthropy), or one on effective uses of video and participatory/collaborative practices for human rights defense with the Southeast Asia-based organization EngageMedia. I'm also concentrating on new frameworks for leadership in our new geopolitical reality, especially through a project supported by the Rockefeller Foundation called "Transformational Change Leadership: Stories of Building a Just Future," which uses stories of leadership process largely from the global south, formerly colonized countries, and lower-resourced communities, to interrogate what it really takes to make change at scale.

But much of what I said about transmedia methodology in the interview still applies: achieving social change and building futures that benefit us all must center on collaborative and partici-patory practice, co-creation, and the lifting of unheard voices and storytelling through multiple channels for community-led social action. As I said then, *"You need narrative to spur social action that resonates with and is relevant to communities that are fighting for positive change. You need to know what's happening at the blood-and-guts-and-feelings level for people – and you need to know what the possibilities and costs of our policies and actions are to actual human beings / Otherwise, what are we fighting for?"* The core work remains the same.

15

Remixing Gender Through Popular Media: Jonathan McIntosh (2017)

Jonathan McIntosh is a media critic, remix artist, and video essayist. He has been deconstructing and recontextualizing popular entertainment for critical and educational purposes since before the invention of YouTube. His current project, The Pop Culture Detective Agency, aims to spark critical discourse through a series of long-form video essays exploring the intersections of politics, masculinity, and entertainment.

"Buffy vs. Edward" helped to establish your reputation as a remix video producer. In some ways, it looks forward to the focus on pop culture and masculinity which has been central to your newest videos. So, can you share some of the thinking behind this now-classic video? What motivated this video? What does it suggest about the relationship of your work to fandom and popular culture more generally? What core political commitments informed this work?

When I saw the first *Twilight* film back in 2008, I was struck by its unmistakably regressive messages about gender. I also noticed that much of the disdain for this movie online was directed at the character of Bella, rather than that of Edward. In general, female characters in entertainment tend to draw more criticism than male characters do.

Often this is because of a combination of sexism and the poor representation of women in a male-dominated media industry. Though, in the case of *Twilight*, the critical focus on Bella's romances seemed especially misguided because Edward is the one depicted engaging in unambiguous stalkerish behavior.

Domestic violence and abuse prevention organizations publish lists of "red flags" to help people identify warning signs in their romantic relationships. Even a casual look at those lists reveals that Edward engages in many "red flag" behaviors over the course of the four *Twilight* books and subsequent movies in the series. These "red flags" include things like extreme jealousy, disregard for personal boundaries, threats of violence, and isolating someone from their friends or family. These controlling behaviors are part of a dangerous and toxic form of masculinity that is often celebrated in entertainment.

When I began constructing my remix video comparing *Twilight*'s conservative gender framing of vampire lore to the more progressive messages embedded in the *Buffy the Vampire Slayer* television show, I made a point of focusing my visual argument on critiquing Edward's behavior. To that end, I removed Bella entirely from the remix and replaced her with footage of Buffy. All of the Buffy clips I used were deliberately chosen to make it appear she was directly responding to Edward's abusive behavior.

My hope with that remix was to re-shape and re-focus online conversations away from Bella's "lack of personality" or "indecisiveness" and back onto Edward's words and actions. Once I released "Buffy vs. Edward" on YouTube[12] in 2009, I was excited to see that the mashup accomplished that goal. All across the Internet, from the *LA Times* to Edward fan fora, I started seeing nuanced conversations pop up about Edward's abusive behaviors.

All of my critical video work uses pop culture as a lens through which I can engage in sociopolitical discussions with fans and general audiences who may not be as familiar with academic theory or texts. My projects are, at their core, critical investigations of the ways entertainment creates meaning in our shared culture.

"Right Wing Radio Duck" brought the political dimensions of your remix practice into much sharper focus and you found yourself responding to some fairly powerful critics within the conservative media sphere. In some ways, you were mapping the emergence of the alt-right ethos that would bring Donald Trump to power. What do you see when you look back on that video and its reception today?

My "Right Wing Radio Duck" remix[13] video was meant as a critique of Glenn Beck in particular, and reactionary right-wing talk radio in general. But, more than that, I wanted to focus on how right-wing demagogues exploit real working-class concerns by scapegoating immigrants and people of color. Many Americans were understandably angry about the bailout of corporate banks after the mortgage crisis of 2007, which left huge subsections of the working poor and middle class out in the cold. Glenn Beck and his ilk preyed on and twisted the very real frustration many Americans were feeling about that economic catastrophe.

I wanted to unequivocally condemn Glenn Beck's racist fearmongering, but didn't want to completely demonize all of his listeners. My goal was to have viewers of my remix come away with a better understanding of why some working folks might be taken in by Tea Party-like rhetoric. It's a bit of a difficult and delicate argument to try to make in any format, but it's especially challenging with remix video because you're so often limited by the source material. That's why I chose Donald Duck as the lens through which to make my critique. Donald seemed especially appropriate for remixing because he was originally created by Disney to represent a frustrated down-on-their-luck Depression-era "everyman." Donald is a hot-headed character. He's easily duped. He's almost always wrong, but critically he's not entirely unsympathetic. In short, he's not a villain. I constructed the remix carefully so we see Donald lose his job, have his house foreclosed on, and then in desperation turn to right-wing radio for answers, only to be driven into a panicked nightmare by racist fearmongering. In my remix, Donald eventually figures out that he's been hoodwinked by right-wing voices that don't really care about him or his struggles.

In terms of the reaction to the remix, I was accused by Beck himself of being part of a union/communist plot funded by Obama to undermine the values of American capitalism. It was ludicrous, but it would have been a lot funnier if it didn't inspire his listeners to start threatening me online. During his heyday on Fox News, Glenn Beck turned out to be a harbinger of things to come. His potent mixture of "tough guy" rhetoric, racist fearmongering, faux populism, and conspiracy theories was nearly identical to what we saw in Donald Trump's 2016 presidential campaign.

You ended up working with Anita Sarkeesian at Feminist Frequency, where you would have seen fairly directly the #gamergate crowd at work. How did those experiences shape your current Pop Culture Detective project?

My experiences while working with Feminist Frequency were definitely a catalyst for the creation of my crowdfunded video series. As you mentioned, I worked as producer and co-writer on the first season of the Tropes vs. Women in Video Games project. During my four years at that job, I became one of gamergate's favorite male targets.

Gamergate, for those who are unfamiliar with it, was a coordinated hate and harassment campaign mostly targeting women involved in video game development and criticism. This online crusade was reactionary in nature and rooted in a particularly virulent strain of anti-feminism. I should note that, since I'm a straight White guy, the type of online abuse I faced was decidedly different (and less intense) than what women endured. Abuse directed at women is often of a sexual nature and includes obsessive stalking and specific threats of intimate violence. When men are harassed online, it usually follows an established pattern of attempted emasculation. Alongside a spade of threats, I was accused of "not being a real man," of being "too sensitive," of being controlled by women, and of course of being gay.

Essentially, I was seen as a traitor to my gender. All this because of my role in critiquing the demeaning and overtly sexualized ways in which female characters are often represented in video games.

The daily insults and abuse hurled at me over social media made it clear that gamergate had as much to do with cultural ideas about hyper-masculinity as it did with women in gaming. Indeed, the two concepts are deeply interconnected. It very quickly became clear to me that the angry young men involved in gamergate saw themselves as protecting video games from the influence of women because they viewed their hobby as one of the "last bastions" of macho manhood.

The gamergate response is perhaps not all that surprising. At every point in history when steps toward equality are won, those gains are met with a reactionary backlash. So, for example, Old West pulp stories saw a surge in popularity which coincided with the rise of movements for women's suffrage. *Men's Adventure* magazines of the 1940s to 1960s were in large part a reaction to gains made by women (and people of color) in the aftermath of World War II. These types of testosterone-infused pulp adventure stories served as a form of "equality escapism" (as I like to call it) for men angered by a changing reality. They offered men a way to retreat to a place where they could engage in regressive power fantasies rooted in White male supremacy. These were narratives where men got to be rugged individualists who dispensed justice from the barrel of a gun (and where those men were rewarded with women). These were fantasy worlds in which men's violence and men's chauvinism were presented as ideal formulations of masculinity.

I'd argue that this same type of macho manhood is mirrored and celebrated in many modern video games. For decades, mainstream video games have leaned on macho power fantasies as a way to appeal to a young straight male demographic. Entitlement to women and women's bodies (and other sexist conventions such as the damsel in distress) played a large part in the type of male fantasies major gaming companies were selling. In the years leading up to gamergate, however, we saw some sectors of the gaming industry very slowly begin taking some steps toward creating better representations of women in their products. A large cross-section of angry young men falsely believe that even modest progress toward gender equality in their favorite entertainment media is something that diminishes them, their power, and their masculinity.

Over and over again, men involved in gamergate would say they were defending their fantasy worlds from "political correctness" and "diversity." They felt some types of video games were important to their identity as men because those games provided them a safe space where "men could be real men again." And they feared that women's input into video games would "feminize" gaming and therefore take away their hyper-masculine fantasy worlds.

The celebration and idealization of macho, violent, and toxic forms of masculinity have always been closely linked to reactionary right-wing politics, and it's an especially potent part of the ideology of hate groups. After gamergate and the rise of Trump, it seemed an important time to start a video series that critically deconstructed toxic representations of manhood in entertainment. That is what my project, The Pop Culture Detective Agency, is all about.

As we turn to your current project, let me ask a question that is the title of one of your videos. What is toxic masculinity and what should we as a society be doing to rein in this particular noxious set of attitudes? Why might educational videos represent one appropriate response to this problem?

"Toxic masculinity" is an important term, but it's often mischaracterized or at least misunderstood in conversation, especially outside of academic settings. The video you're referring to is my attempt to clarify the meaning of the term and hopefully spark more constructive conversations.

As I said in my video on the topic,[14] "toxic masculinity" refers to a particular set of harmful actions and cultural practices. It's marked by things like emotional detachment and hyper-competitiveness. It's connected to the sexual objectification of women, as well as other predatory sexual behaviors, and it's also linked very closely with aggression, intimidation, and violence.

It's important to note that "toxic masculinity" is not a condemnation of men or manhood in general. There is nothing toxic about being a man, but some men act in toxic ways. In other words, toxic masculinity is not something that men are, but rather it's something that some men do. Which means that we, as men, can choose not to participate in that toxic behavior and instead choose other more empathetic, cooperative, compassionate forms of manhood.

In terms of why educational videos like mine are useful, the hope is that they can help get us on the same page. It's very hard, if not impossible, to have these difficult conversations when critical words are terms so widely misunderstood or misrepresented.

Let me ask another blunt and straightforward question. Why should we care what kinds of representation of masculinity run through popular culture? Shouldn't we be more concerned with actual male behavior in everyday life, rather than the masculinity of wizards and stormtroopers?

I believe we should be concerned with both. The truth is that personal expressions of masculinity and media representations of manhood are not separate and distinct: they're deeply interconnected. Media and culture have a cyclical relationship; media influences culture and, conversely, culture influences media. Obviously, that doesn't mean we're all mindlessly mimicking what we see on television, but one thing media is very good at doing is shaping our worldview.

One of my favorite feminist theorists, bell hooks, connects the dots succinctly; she says: "Popular culture is where the pedagogy is, it's where the learning is happening." She's right. Our cultural ideas about what it means to be a man are heavily influenced by entertainment. Of course, schools, families, and religious and political institutions all play important roles, but, for better or worse, mass media are a primary area where our cultural ideals of manhood are shaped and reaffirmed. This is why I believe it's critical for us to interrogate what those Stormtroopers and Wizards are teaching us about masculinity.

All media have embedded messages and values, whether producers and filmmakers intend to include them or not. When it comes to myths about manhood, some of the most common ideas we see infused in entertainment often pass under the radar because they reflect current cultural norms. These include myths such as: men are naturally aggressive and violent; men who express vulnerability are weak; manhood is earned through physical competition and conquest; men's sexist behavior is biologically driven. These messages are limiting and harmful for a whole host of reasons, not least of which being because they reinforce the false notion that toxic behaviors, practices, and attitudes are normal, natural, and even inevitable, for men.

The reality, of course, is that men are capable of transformation. This is why we need media that model alternative formulations of masculinity in which men are shown openly communicating their feelings and vulnerabilities, practicing de-escalation tactics, and embracing empathetic responses to conflicts and challenges.

Media change us – sometimes for better, sometimes for worse. They have incredible power to alter our perceptions, shape our worldview, and transform our identities. Media can trap us in old ways of thinking or open up exciting new social possibilities. My long-form video essays are focused on challenging media that do the former, and elevating media that do the latter.

Today, the phrase – men's movement – has often been co-opted into a misogynistic backlash against "political correctness" in general, and feminism in particular, making it harder to speak as a male ally of feminism. How would you characterize the perspective you bring to these videos? What works provide you with the intellectual framework you draw upon in this work?

As I mentioned above, my work is very much influenced by feminist writers such as bell hooks. Back in 1984, hooks boldly advocated for a feminism that included men. Her second book, *Feminist Theory: From Margin to Center*, includes this passage, which has stuck with me and provided a framework for my own work on masculinity. She notes, "Men are not exploited or oppressed by sexism, but there are ways in which they suffer as a result of it." Her point about how the social system of patriarchy privileges men, while simultaneously harming us by robbing us of our humanity, is a foundational one for my Pop Culture Detective Agency project. Hooks expands on this perspective in her excellent book *The Will to Change: Men, Masculinity, and Love*. That book is, incidentally, the first thing I always recommend to guys who are just beginning their journey into what feminism means for men. I find it both critical and inspiring that hooks calls for men to be held accountable while still remaining deeply compassionate to our struggles as men.

Another important influence for me has been the work of sociologist Allan G. Johnson. who wrote a book called *Unraveling Our Patriarchal Legacy*. I've found his insights about how social systems and individuals are interconnected (neither exists without the other) to be particularly helpful in my research and criticism. R. W. Connell's academic writings on *Masculinities* are also very useful for my work. She argues that there are many types and formulations of masculinity, all of which exist within a hierarchy of "masculinities."

As you alluded to in your question, my perspective is fundamentally different from that of those who call themselves "Men's Rights Activists," or MRAs. There are now hundreds of men with shockingly popular YouTube channels and social media followings who purport to care about men's issues. Unfortunately, most of them are indeed coming from a decidedly reactionary place which oozes hatred for feminism and is steeped in a palpable resentment of women. These guys are openly advocating for a return to the hypermasculine male supremacist values of decades past. They're upset that our culture is slowly evolving in terms of gender, and they're determined to resist this social progress. The dark irony is that many of the things MRAs point to as being problems for men in our society (suicide rates, combat deaths, life expectancy, etc.) are not a result of feminism or "discrimination against men" but are instead a byproduct of the social system of patriarchy.

Instead of working to find real solutions to these issues (which would require a measure of self-criticism and self-transformation), MRAs are hell-bent on blaming feminism in particular, and women in general. In many ways, my video essays are a direct response to the popularity of the poisonous MRA prospective. My hope is that, by compassionately addressing the emotional harm men and boys face as a result of patriarchal pressures in our culture, I can reach some of the guys who are hurting and perhaps keep some from joining reactionary movements.

You celebrate *Steven Universe* for offering a more positive role model for young boys. What is it doing that seems distinctive and progressive to you?

When I first saw *Steven Universe* on Cartoon Network, I was pleasantly surprised by its subversive themes and plotlines. A lot has been written about the show's progressive values, and rightly so; it centers powerful women and contains relatively unambiguous positive depictions of queer relationships. Last year, I produced two videos focusing on something that gets a little less attention: the downright revolutionary ways in which men and boys are represented.

One of those video essays explores Steven's superpowers.[15] This is an adventure show about a boy with superpowers derived from an interstellar gemstone, which he uses to summon a magical shield. It's rare to see a boy hero given a largely defensive weapon instead of an offensive one. Indeed, Steven's main contributions to his superhero team are shielding, protecting, and healing his teammates. Those are all traits traditionally associated with women, in fantasy fiction. But beyond that, I argue Steven has an additional less obvious superpower which is even more fundamental to his character and to the show's values. And that's Steven's empathy, which plays a critical role in de-escalation and conflict resolution throughout the series. Again, that's something exceptionally rare to see with boy heroes in these kinds of narratives.

My other *Steven Universe* video[16] focuses on emotional expression. In Hollywood, men are typically not shown expressing feelings of vulnerability, at least not outside of a very narrow set of traumatic circumstances, such as when a loved one dies. *Steven Universe* doesn't play by those rules – on that show, men are regularly depicted as expressing a wide range of feelings in response to all kinds of social situations.

Whenever I talk about emotional expression in male characters, I make a point of emphasizing the "expression" part. Most male characters are, of course, written to have feelings and emotions on some level. It's not uncommon for male heroes to harbor a deep-seated inner pain. However, that pain is usually left unspoken. We as audiences are meant to understand that male heroes experience intense feelings, but that turmoil is framed as something they must keep hidden. They're very rarely shown openly communicating or vocalizing their vulnerabilities. The emotions that men on the big screen are allowed to express are anger and rage. And those emotions are typically closely aligned with acts of violent revenge which are framed as a form of vigilante justice. Needless to say, this is the very definition of being emotionally unhealthy.

Steven Universe is the exact opposite. As I mentioned, the show is absolutely packed with men and boys who are open and vocal about expressing their emotions. So, for example, everyone in the show cries. Men and boys are shown crying in most episodes, and, more importantly, these tears are never presented as a sign of weakness. In fact, tears serve to communicate an impressively wide range of emotions, from joy to concern, from despair to pride, from frustration to love.

Steven and his father Greg are also not afraid of being physically affectionate with those around them, and not just when it comes to family or romantic partners either. Steven openly admits to being afraid, and he is never shamed for expressing that fear. Unlike many other coming-of-age stories about boy heroes, Steven's growth does not hinge on learning to "conquer his fear." Instead, Steven learns that fear is a natural and useful emotion, something he should listen to in order to help keep himself and those he cares about safe. All of this is exceptionally rare for television. It's especially notable given that *Steven Universe* is an animated series aimed at younger audiences.

To what degree are the myths of masculinity you discuss inherited unconsciously as part of the genre formulas passed down from earlier generations of media makers? To what degree is masculinity being reimagined and reasserted today in equally destructive terms?

Certainly, there are a whole bunch of regressive ideas about masculinity baked into many long-running traditions in genre fiction. Hollywood's current rush to remake and reboot franchises from decades past has meant we've seen images of aggressive manhood reproduced in uncritical ways. Over the past decade, superhero movies have taken over the box office. That genre in particular lends itself to portrayals of manhood in which physical intimidation, violence, and vengeance are framed as effective and heroic forms of conflict resolution for men. Incidentally, that goes for both small interpersonal conflicts as well as larger intergalactic conflicts.

We've also seen some entertainment that I'd categorize as being part of a conservative backlash against progressive or feminist gains. I already mentioned that some popular gaming franchises are especially guilty in this regard. Recent films by directors such as Michael Bay, Zack Snyder, and Peter Berg would also fit into this category since many of their productions tend to unapologetically celebrate aggressive versions of hypermasculinity.

On the whole, though, I do think a lot of Hollywood writers and media makers are much more aware of the potentially harmful conventions and clichés in their work these days. Unfortunately, the relatively high level of media literacy on the production side hasn't translated into much in the way of new or subversive storylines for male characters. What we get instead is an enormous amount of lampshading.

Lampshading is a writers' trick wherein media makers deliberately call attention to a dissonant, clichéd, or stereotypical aspect of their own production within the text itself. It's basically a wink in the direction of the audience. Lampshading is often used as a way for media makers to acknowledge troubling or toxic gender representations in their production, but then continue to uncritically indulge in those depictions. Lampshaded dialog can make writers seem clever, self-aware, and even self-critical, while still largely sticking to Hollywood traditions. This then tends to make a piece of media seem more progressive or subversive than it really is.

My latest video essay, "The Adorkable Misogyny of the Big Bang Theory,"[17] details how ironic lampshading is employed in comedies and sitcoms as a way to let nerdy "nice guys" off the hook for a wide range of creepy behaviors. But lampshading is increasingly used in dramas as well. It's one of Joss Whedon's favorite writing techniques: he'll often write humorous lines of dialog to point out macho behaviors in his male characters, only to then have them keep engaging in those same behaviors. So, for example, there's a scene in *Avengers: Age of Ultron* in which the male heroes take turns trying to lift Thor's hammer. The witty writing acknowledges that these men are involved in what amounts to an extended "dick measuring" contest over who is the stronger superhero. There's even a line where Black Widow makes fun of them all for it. In another Marvel movie from different directors, *Captain America: Civil War*, Black Widow asks point blank whether the male hero really wants to "punch his way out" of a difficult situation. But again, even though the problem is explicitly acknowledged in the text, nothing fundamentally changes in terms of how those male characters are depicted; they still solve the majority of their problems by punching other men in the face.

So I'd argue that, while many Hollywood writers are on some level aware that toxic and violent masculinity is an issue, they either have no alternative or they don't really believe it's a big enough deal to take seriously – preferring instead to acknowledge the issue and then double down on the same old formulas. The end result of all these forms of replication is the same: a market flooded with images of violent macho manhood, some done with a wink to the audience, but precious few representations that directly challenge those hypermasculine ideals.

So, while the clichés of genre traditions are more readily acknowledged today, I'd argue that media makers are still trapped. However, it's not that difficult to become unstuck. It just requires a willingness to defy audience expectations. I will say that there are a few exceptions to the rule where filmmakers do embrace atypical and empathetic versions of heroic masculinity. I recently made a video essay about the *Harry Potter* spin-off,[18] *Fantastic Beasts and Where to Find Them*, in which I posit that the protagonist, Newt Scamander, is a welcome subversion of traditional male action-adventure heroes.

If you had the attention of people working in genre entertainment today (and I am sure you do), what would you most want them to learn from watching your videos?

First and foremost that their work isn't just entertainment; media can have enormous impacts on people's belief structures, worldview, attitudes, and sometimes behaviors. In various times and places around the world, the role of storyteller has been a sacred and revered position because their job includes the responsibility of passing on lessons, values, and cultural identity to a younger generation. Media makers are the most influential storytellers of today, and, like it or not, there is a lot of power that comes with that job.

And it's possible to do things differently even within the confines of a major studio production. *The Martian*, for example, was a widely successful, thrilling, edge-of-your-seat blockbuster, and one that remarkably contains absolutely no images of men solving problems with violence. All conflicts are solved through the use of science, cooperation, and human ingenuity.

As I mentioned above, another successful movie with an unconventional male hero is *Fantastic Beasts and Where to Find Them*. Newt performs a refreshingly atypical form of masculinity. He's sincere, nurturing, empathetic, and sensitive. And, crucially, that sensitivity is framed as a strength rather than a weakness.

It may sound clichéd to say that "with great power comes great responsibility," but it's true, and it's especially true when it comes to Hollywood. Media makers have a responsibility to be careful and intentional about the messages and values embedded in their stories. If producers and filmmakers are willing to take the risk of showing emotionally vulnerable, communicative, empathetic versions of leading-manhood, I think they'll find a large audience out there that is hungry for those alternative depictions of masculinity.

Reflections

Over the past few years, we've seen some exciting movement toward better media representation around gender, race, and sexuality. Unfortunately, this progress continues to be met with public tempertantrums from a subsection of angry (mostly) male fans. Cyber mobs and harassment campaigns have coalesced around new entries in popular franchises such as *Ghostbusters*, Marvel Comics, DC's *Titans*, *Doctor Who*, and *Star Wars* over decisions to cast women and people of color in iconic roles. While a "culture war" around mass media is nothing new, what is noteworthy is the degree to which we've seen far-right voices opportunistically use social media as a way to leverage fan backlash and channel the rage into right-wing political movements.

As part of our interview a couple of years back, we briefly talked about the rise of so-called Men's Rights Activists, or MRAs. These groups aren't particularly interested in helping struggling men, and instead use social media to agitate for a return to a time when male entitlement and male dominance were unquestioned social norms and women were largely thought of as a subordinate domestic class. Nostalgia for White hypermasculinity has also proven to be a key ingredient in recruitment for other far-right, reactionary, White nationalist, and fascist groups.

I recently made a video essay, "How *The Last Jedi* Defies Expectations about Male Heroes," where I examined the reactionary backlash aimed at that film. I pointed out that, although outraged superfans have a litany of complaints, one common accusation is that *The Last Jedi* is "feminist propaganda" and part of a conspiracy by the Disney corporation to emasculate male heroes in entertainment. That type of "anti-male" media conspiracy theory has been echoed by reactionary social media celebrities such as Milo Yiannopoulos, Carl Benjamin, Ben Shapiro, and Gavin McInnes, just to name a few. These figures have cynically latched on to fan outrage and deliberately stoked the flames in order to push their far-right ideologies.

The Last Jedi conspiracy theorists falsely claim the film is "anti-male" because, in their view, Luke Skywalker was stripped of his status as the most powerful warrior in the galaxy, Finn was forced to take lessons in justice and morality from a preachy woman of color, and Poe Dameron was transformed from a badass "never-tell-me-the-odds" pilot into a doormat who's demeaned by bossy female leaders. Needless to say, these reactionary interpretations of the film's messages are deeply misguided. As I explain in my video essay on the topic, what really happens in *The Last Jedi* is that flawed male characters learn important lessons from the women in their lives. They then internalize those lessons and become better, more effective heroes because of it.

My Pop Culture Detective Agency project is designed to combat reactionary backlash and provide an alternative perspective on masculinity in media. In my video essays, I demonstrate that, far from diminishing, demonizing, or erasing men, more inclusive and diverse media representations are good for men: first, because they can help men – especially straight White men – to identify and empathize with women, people of color, and LGBT characters on screen; and, second, because the changing media ecosystem can create openings for more dynamic male characters who are allowed to express a wider array of vulnerable emotions.

16

Charting Documentary's Futures:
William Uricchio (2016)

William Uricchio is Professor of Comparative Media Studies at MIT in the US, as well as at Utrecht University in the Netherlands. He is principal investigator of the MIT Open Documentary Lab, which explores the frontiers of interactive and participatory reality-based storytelling. His work explores the frontiers of new media, at times using a historical lens (old media when they were new, such as nineteenth-century television) and at times by working with interactive and algorithmically generated media forms (interactive documentaries and games, in particular). Uricchio has received numerous awards for his work, including Guggenheim, Humboldt, and Fulbright research fellowships, the Berlin Prize, and, most recently, the Mercator fellowship.

Most recent accounts of the state of journalism in the digital age have emphasized the bad news – describing all of the risks and challenges – but your report, *Mapping the Intersection of Two Cultures: Interactive Documentary and Digital Journalism*, also describes some of the new opportunities and the ways in which newspapers and other legacy media organizations are restructuring themselves to take advantage of the changing media environment. So, what do you see as some of the opportunities for new kinds of news and documentary production emerging at the present moment?

Yes, lots of doom and gloom out there! It helps to take a more analytical approach to the problems facing quality journalism, and that has indeed resulted in finding a number of opportunities that can be of tangible use to legacy organizations at a moment of change.

I'd like to begin by invoking what's always struck me as one of James Carey's great insights into how we think about communication. Carey notes that we too often focus only on the transmission of information – and in "we," I include academics as well as journalists. And with this narrow focus, we often neglect communication's ritual dimension. Carey's notion of ritual entails much more than the habit of reading a newspaper with breakfast, or closing out the evening news broadcast with tomorrow's weather (yes, no matter how dismal the news, there will be a tomorrow!). Instead, he understands ritual as creating shared concepts and habits by drawing on participation, sharing, association, and fellowship.

Facebook and Buzzfeed, while a little erratic on the transmission side, understand this, and they and others like them have hard-wired ritual into their systems. And their user-base understands it as well. At a fundamental level, the opportunities for new kinds of journalism and documentary production turn not so much on the availability of new technologies, but rather on the use of those technologies to bring ritual into the picture. In other words, simply putting news content, no matter how good, online with the hope of expanding audience reach and engagement misses the point. Instead, finding ways to enhance user participation, to intensify immersive experiences, and to encourage sharing and community-building all help to embrace the ritual dimension noted by Carey. It's not so much about the de-profession-alization of the news (in fact, our study focuses on quality journalism), as it is the expansion of news as a process that includes a community of participants, expanded textual forms, and a reconfigured production pipeline. Participation leads to greater engagement, inclusiveness, relevance ... and better-informed communities.

Despite its rock-solid appearance, journalistic convention has transformed over the past several hundred years, and today we face an accelerated rate of change. Whereas, for much of the twentieth century, journalism served as a definer of truths, today's high-connectivity and intensive information flow have enabled new expectations and given journalism a new agenda, helping it to inform the connection between publics and sources, shaping conversations in addition to defining truths....

In some ways, your report is bringing together two forms of media production – journalism and documentary – that have historically been understood as distinct, even though they have both sought to get the public to be more aware and more responsive to urgent social conditions. These two fields often operate according to different professional ideologies and different standards of ethics. Why have they stayed separate for so long, and in what ways are we starting to see some convergence between them?

If I had to boil the difference between the journalistic and documentary traditions down to a caricature, I'd say that, since the mid-1920s, journalism has been bound by a commitment to "facts" and documentary by a commitment to "truth." OK – both are slippery words, and the two are not irreconcilable. But an insistence on the "facts" as journalistic fact-checkers define them can sometimes leave a larger truth hanging in the balance; and the pursuit of "truth" can call upon innovative and imaginative strategies that would be nixed by any fact-checker worth her salt.

The distinction between the two is deeply rooted in institutional history, with the several-hundred-year-old "fourth estate" – as Carlyle called the press – finding a protected niche in places like the US Constitution, and playing a fundamental role in governance in most cultures. In this context, an insistence upon verifiable data makes sense.

Documentary, by contrast – at least if we stick to the classic telling of the tale – emerged in the film medium in the form of a re-enacted, character-based drama that strove for a greater truth (Flaherty's 1926

213

Moana), or what John Grierson later called "the creative treatment of actuality."

Journalism has been long bound by professionalization, certification, codes of behavior, and rules, while documentary has thrived as an eclectic intention-based assemblage of experiments (mostly formal), techniques (mostly narrative), and effects (mostly generating insight and empathy). Epistemological differences, institutional differences, media differences ... even differences in which part of the academy they are studied ... no wonder the two traditions seem to be worlds apart!

As I said, this description is something of a caricature, and these two nonfiction storytelling traditions have at times overlapped, especially in the domain of essayistic journalism or places like *Frontline* – where documentary makers hew to journalistic rules – and the *New York Times*, the *Guardian*, and *The Economist*, all of which have in-house documentary units. But even here, an insistence on fact provides the bottom line for a story to count as journalistic, even if drawing heavily on documentary notions of story, character, and engagement.

So, what changed, and why do these two forms now seem more open to sharing with one another? The steady shift of users of both forms to mobile, digital platforms; the emergence of interactive and visually immersive forms of telling stories; and the popularity of operations like Facebook, Buzzfeed, and Vice – these have all put pressure on those who simply wanted to put the printed page, television feed or 16mm film online. Traditional newspaper readership and news viewership, like documentary viewership, are not only declining ... but aging. And while troubling from a business perspective, this decline is of far greater concern to the needs of an informed public and the civic process.

True, the just-mentioned digital startups have embraced "news" as part of their remit (and, in the process, raided legacy journalistic organizations and made some very impressive hires), and some of them can claim vast communities of young users, but the quality, context, and mission of that embrace are neither clear nor consistent.

Indeed, the surfeit of information and the poor ratio of signal to noise that we are experiencing "out there" makes the work of the tried and true legacy journalistic operations more important than ever.

It's here that the new documentary provides a valuable set of assets for the journalistic endeavor, offering ways for it to keep core values while embracing a more user-centric and participatory ethos that makes the most of the new media ecosystem.

Documentary's relative freedom from institutional constraint has enabled its makers to experiment in ways that are difficult for traditional journalists. Moreover, as journalism becomes more of a curator of information and shaper of conversations, documentary's demonstrated ability to contextualize and explain through well-chosen instances has proven newly relevant. The interactive documentaries produced to date offer a compendium of approaches, interfaces, user experiences, tools, and even strategies for working with crowd-sourced and co-created content, all of which journalists can assess, draw from and transform.

So, I guess I would say that, by finding themselves in the same boat, both journalists and documentarians have discovered commonalities of purpose and technique. Interactive documentary is fast developing a repertoire of techniques that work well in today's "digital first" and increasingly participatory environment, and digital journalism still commands considerable reputation and audience reach.

The dust has not settled, of course, but as we work toward journalism's and documentary's next iterations, the one thing that is clear is that they have more in common now than at any other point in their histories. And the best indication of this commonality takes the form of the many interactive features, data-driven stories, and even immersive approaches to information organization that have been appearing with increasing regularity on the digital sites of leading journalism organizations.

You argue that the story should dictate the form, yet many aspects of the form of American journalism – the inverted pyramid, for example, and the core shape of the lead paragraph – have remain

fixed without regard to the story. Some traditional journalists would argue that these formulas allow for quick production of news and for interoperability amongst collaborators. So, how do you make the case to such traditionalists for a broader range of different kinds of news stories?

Journalistic form has changed continually over the centuries, some elements sticking and some new ones displacing old. Things like headlines and the inverted pyramid appeared for the reasons you mention, plus enabling readers to orient themselves and, when required, make quick work of the day's news. They work well and seem to be sticking in the digital environment, arguably a predecessor of the "listicle."

We are witnessing an evolutionary process, but one that is accelerated as much because of a change in the use of media technologies as because of a change in the larger information situation of the user and her attendant expectations. The move from print and broadcast to digital platforms has brought with it many new affordances, and while traditionalists can stick with techniques that have proven effective with the printed page or news clip (rightly arguing that the digital can easily incorporate the page and the clip), digital media technologies – including the small mobile screens that currently loom large in most user experiences – have been put to many other uses that could enhance both journalism and user engagement.

To be honest, I don't know of any journalistic organizations, no matter how traditional, that have failed in their digital operations to make use of embedded links, or auto-generated links to past stories, or an array of user tracking applications. These have changed the presentation of news and relationship to the user, just as digital processes have changed the workflow within the newsroom. Their impact can be read as subtle or profound, depending on one's point of view. But even the most traditional journalistic organization is acutely aware of Vice, Buzzfeed, and Facebook's Instant Articles initiative, their fast-growing market share, and their appeal to younger readers.

Our report's conclusion that 'story dictates form' simply means that there is no 'one size fits all' convention for storytelling. The digital has brought with it an expanded set of approaches, has offered new – and digitally relevant – options. The report says that, now that we have more choices, we should use them critically and strategically – not just jump on the bandwagon of the new (or stick fetishistically to the old). A data-rich story might benefit from visualizations, and even personalization through interaction, whereas the same techniques would add little to a personal profile. The new is no more a panacea than the old, but it does offer expanded choice.

But, at a moment when the media ecosystem is fast changing, with consequences financial, informational, and generational, we need to understand better the affordances of the new. This by no means entails discarding lessons hard learnt over centuries of journalistic practice, but it does mean not necessarily sticking to paper- and broadcast-based habits just because they happen to be well established. And, particularly as the role of the user continues to grow, journalists and documentary makers need actively to consider the fit of form and content rather than slipping into inherited defaults....

Some of the more interactive elements you describe take time to develop, and this means slowing down the pace of news production and taking a long-view perspective of social issues. How can we reconcile this with the 24-hours-a-day news cycle and other factors which are speeding up the production, circulation, and consumption of news?

Temporality is one of the most intriguing dimensions of today's journalism scene. On one hand, Twitter and other services have reduced the lag between event and report to just about nothing. OK, these aren't traditional fact-checked reports, but in the aggregate they tend to give a first heads-up about breaking news, and even legacy journalism is making increasing use of tweets in their coverage. On the other, in a world bubbling with reports of all kinds and qualities, the need for context, perspective, and plain old pattern recognition has never been greater.

The traditional 24-hour cycle is under siege from both sides: it can't keep pace with networked digital sources, and has generally left the reflective contextualizing work to occasional investigative and feature stories or to specialized venues such as magazines and programs like *Frontline*. All to say that the time cycles that have worked for the better part of a century no longer seem to be addressing public needs.

The *Guardian* was quick to try to redress this, embracing breaking news (even minute-by-minute blog reports of the Republican and Democratic presidential debates or the Academy Awards), carrying on with the traditional 24-hour cycle, and redoubling its feature work. And it's in this last context that they have carried out much of their interactive work. The verdict is still out on how legacy organizations will deal with this challenge – having it all, *Guardian*-style, won't necessarily work for everyone.

The *Guardian*'s experimental stance has yielded some great innovative work that blurs the divide between immediate and long-term journalism. "The Counted" hews to the 24-hour cycle, but aggregates the daily updates, encouraging readers to look for patterns (age, ethnicity, location, etc.) as the data collect over the course of the year. It harvests the daily news, folds it into a larger context, offers analytic tools, and in the process renders the normally hyper-local into something of national import. In fact, it reveals that many incidents are not reported, or are reported so locally that the rest of the country has no idea of the scale of the problem.

So, experiments like these that complicate the familiar temporalities and logics of journalism offer signs that multiple news cycles can intertwine, and actually contribute to one another, to deliver a powerful set of insights that would otherwise be missed.

More generally, though, you are right: most interactives are like feature stories, "evergreens" capable of drawing in users well after the initial publication date. And, in this, they are particularly good at contextualizing, explaining, and offering multiple points of view.

For the moment, they are labor-intensive, but developers are sharing bits of code and tools among themselves, flexible content management systems and even templates are beginning to appear, and in general the process is accelerating. Some thought leaders fear that these efficiencies could go too far, that the innovation that has driven new kinds of user experience will reify into rigid one-size-fits-all templates. And, indeed, the front office has a habit of thinking about the bottom line, and these are still early days in terms of expanded story form. But I mention this simply to say that it's clear that these efficiencies can and will speed up the process, even though it is essential for leading organizations to continue exploring and building innovative story technologies that work with the platforms most familiar to the public.

On the documentary side, the American public has probably never had access to as many different documentaries as they do now – more are playing on television, more are getting theatrical runs, more are playing on the festival circuit, more are available through online platforms. So, how has this context impacted the ways documentary producers work today? How do they stand out in a cluttered environment? They are under increased pressure from funders to demonstrate their impact, but how do they insure impact in such a complicated media environment?

It's been a curious time for the documentary form. It's being pushed on one side by the interactive, immersive, location-based forms that our report explores, where the boundaries are being redefined through new technologies, techniques, and empowered users. And, on the other side, the traditional linear form is blurring thanks to a broad spectrum of reality television, from *Animal Planet*'s programming to series such as *MythBusters*. These predictably formatted programs technically hew to Grierson's definition, but for the most part seem like extreme dilutions of documentary's capacity to engage meaningfully with the world.

Meanwhile, there is indeed a lot of excellent linear documentary out there. I've been to a couple of remarkable festivals over the past few months – but, sad to say, very little of what I've seen will ever be seen again, unless it's at another festival or by very adventurous users of Netflix. The more socially critical and engaged, the poorer the opportunities for theatrical or televisual distribution ... and it's still early days in terms of the various modalities of Internet distribution.

The developments that we've been tracking address the "attention" problem in a couple of ways. First, they are in many cases designed for the viewing platforms that seem increasingly dominant: smartphones and tablets – that is, relatively small mobile screens with touch interfaces. In this sense, they are digital-native productions, making use of links, user interventions, etc., already well understood from everyday encounters with these technologies. They take the form of a new vernacular, rather than repurposing the older forms of dramatic narrative film, television, and the long-form story.

Second, in a number of cases, they attempt to be immersive. This might take as extreme a form as Karim Ben Khelifa's *The Enemy*, which uses Oculus Rift to bring an interview to life; or as simple a form as *Question Bridge* (Hank Willis Thomas, Kamal Sinclair, Chris Johnson, and Bayeté Ross Smith), which lets users follow their interests by controlling the configuration of questions and answers.

And, as this suggests, third, a high degree of customization is often possible, as users make decisions about what they want to see, which characters or perspectives they want to follow, or where they want to dive more deeply.

These approaches to attention also, unfortunately, make the lack of attention quite visible. Whereas linear documentaries continue to flow along regardless of whether one is watching, asleep, or in the next room making a sandwich, interactives usually stop cold the moment that one has stopped interacting with them. And, in a world of data tracking, that is not always good news for interactives. Attention can be more sharply measured, but the metrics regimes between linear and interactive aren't necessarily compatible.

I find impact a fraught area in general, and in particular in the case of interactives, where we have tended to extend the logics of assessing fixed linear texts to texts with a very different set of conditions and affordances. There has been a recent spate of impact assessment studies that have essentially (and often unknowingly) worked in parallel with the television industry, where, as Philip Napoli puts it, interest in exposure has been replaced by interest in engagement ...

Anyway, in the more refined world of academics and foundations concerned with social change, the same basic shift in thinking is under way. How can we use the new tools available to us (Twitter feeds and Facebook mentions) to better understand engagement, impact, and social change?

It's a fair question, of course, and there are good reasons to ask what kind of impact a documentary had and what we can learn in order to improve down the road. But, at the moment, we seem caught up in defaults that largely extend the thinking of the broadcast past and its obsession with comparative metrics and standardization, redoubling it with the data trails users of digital media leave behind. And that, it seems to me, does a great disservice to the affordances of the inter-active forms we've been investigating.

There is a world of difference between, on one hand, taking a guided tour of a city, where one sits back and listens to an informed and compelling tale, and, on the other, wandering through the city on one's own, where there is much greater latitude in terms of where to direct attention and different requirements for engagement. I'm not (yet) convinced that the latter experience can be measured on the same stand-ardized customer satisfaction form as the former. So, while I am by no means averse to assessment, I guess I'd say that the verdict is still out on best impact-assessment practices for the interactive space, though many of my colleagues seem comfortable with tweaking the tools developed for fixed linear experiences and porting them over to interactives....

Your lab is focused on "open documentaries." What does this phrase mean to you and what are some examples of how these techniques have been deployed?

Open.... We use this term for a couple of reasons. One important cluster of motives comes from our institutional setting: MIT.

Back in the 1960s and 1970s, Ricky Leacock, probably best known for his work with direct cinema, was increasingly involved in developing a film technology that would put the tools of documentary production into everyone's hands. His work with sound Super 8mm was, we now know, doomed by the soon-to-emerge technology of portable video, but his endeavor was right on target: how can we take the next step from "direct cinema?" How can we empower the documentary subject to take up the means of representation and tell their own story? How can we enable widespread participation in the documentary project, opening up the filmmaker–subject dynamic in important ways?

A second factor is the work of Glorianna Davenport's group at the Media Lab. Starting in the 1980s, Glorianna and her team developed some remarkably sophisticated interactive platforms – conceptual equivalents of what we are still doing today. The difference was that projects like Elastic Charles involved stacks of computers and laser disks to implement – they were technology-intensive in the worst way. But they opened up the user's ability to explore an issue, to assemble the parts in ways that made sense to them.

A third MIT-related invocation of "open" comes from the legacy of people such as Hal Ableson, Gerald Sussman, Richard Stallman, and others, who were instrumental in founding initiatives such as the free software movement and Creative Commons. With a goal of opening up code and creative work for sharing and creative reiteration, their work helped us to appreciate the importance of opening up the processes, techniques, and even tools behind the screen, and of incorporating the principles of sharing and participation into the bones of the documentary project. Together, Leacock's participatory technology, Davenport's interactive texts, and Ableson et al.'s sharing and learning economy all contributed key elements to our work. Sure, today's widespread and networked mobile technologies and a tech-savvy population are important, but more important are the underlying principles. Understanding them and fighting the good fight to keep and expand them are essential, especially if we seek to enhance critical engagement and encourage widespread participation in the project of representing and changing the world.

Beyond "open" as an adjective, we also use it as a verb, since our lab's task is to open debate, to open the documentary form to new participants, to explore the possibilities of new technologies, and to understand the expressive capacities of new textual possibilities. It's a big agenda, and in part means revisiting documentary's past to 'liberate' it from the film medium (the documentary ethos, we argue in Moments of Innovation, has been around for centuries and taken many different media forms).

And finally, consistent with the spirit of CMS that binds your and my histories together, we do our best to open our lab's doors and ideas to anyone who might benefit from our work ... and, at the same time, to be open to and learn from the many different experiences out there in the world.

This all hits documentary in several ways. First, more people than ever before are equipped to make documentaries, to reflect on and give form to their ideas and observations. High-definition video cameras are built into most smartphones, and Vine and YouTube upload rates suggest that producing moving images is increasingly the norm. Second, networked distribution enables unprecedented global reach. Third, the tools for designing interactive and participatory texts have never been so accessible, in the senses of both easy and free. And, meanwhile, interactivity has been increasingly normalized in our encounters with situated texts – that is, we have become comfortable navigating our way through texts and contexts, effectively constructing our own meta-texts (whether on our mobile devices, audio-visual systems, or DVDs). This all adds up to an incentive to think about newly enabled users, new ways of telling stories, and new ways of connecting with one another.

The report's focus on immersion as a dimension of news and documentary may be new to many readers, despite the *New York*

Times's recent venture into virtual reality. So, can you share a bit more about the current state of immersive journalism and why you think this is a trend which we should be paying attention to, rather than a passing fad? How would you respond to fears that immersion is more a tool for shaping emotional response, rather than a resource for fostering reasoned argument? Can news stories be both immersive (and thus framed by a particular vantage point) and objective, in the traditional sense of the term?

To answer your last question first, if we take immersive technology in the form of VR to mean 360-degree, 3D imaging systems (there is a lot of slippage in the meanings of both 'immersive' and 'VR'), I actually think that it's easier to be less subjective, or at least to circumvent the problem of a particular point-of-view common to linear narratives in film, video, words, and even traditional photography.

One of its affordances as a medium, and a great advantage or disadvantage depending on one's goals, is that VR offers a surfeit of information. This makes directing the user's attention or "constructing the gaze" a difficult task. Indeed, it's one of the reasons VR storytelling is still in its infancy: how to impose structure and direction, other than to mimic film conventions? In these early days, VR storytelling feels a lot like the first decade of cinematic storytelling, when the conventions from another medium (theatre) informed the endeavors of a new medium still finding its feet.

I recently experienced *Waves of Grace*, a terrific project about an Ebola survivor whose immunity offers a story of hope, made by Gabo Arora and Chris Milk for the UN in collaboration with Vice Media. It's clear that the makers have a point of view, a story that they want to communicate. And while reader-response theory tells us that viewers can and will make their own meanings from texts, in this case, the viewer has 360 degrees at his disposal, and in my case, I'm pretty sure that I constructed a counter-narrative, possibly abusing my freedom to look around, to look "behind" or opposite the makers' focus, to see things they weren't talking about and perhaps didn't want to take up.

More objective? I think the viewer has more options, can look around at what would normally be "off-screen space" in a film or video image, and that means viewers have greater latitude in figuring out not only what they are supposed to look at, but also the larger setting and context.

The bigger issue, according to some research, is that we might be processing these encounters the same way we do real-world experiences, and not the way we process film or photography or words. That is, we might be processing them as experience, not representation ... I think immersive experiences put a new twist on the old 'showing–telling' distinction. Showing is far more difficult to contain than telling, seems more impactful in terms of how it is experienced and remembered, and, as Confucius tells us, can be re-told in thousands of words and thus in countless ways. VR takes showing to the next level, not only always presenting us with an excess of information, but, in so doing, forcing us to attend to only a small portion of what is available, and giving us that information as experience. I think it would be difficult to argue that it is a tool for reasoned argument – the abstraction of words and numbers is still best for that, with image and sound beginning the slippery slope to affect. (I guess that's what the Reformation was all about!)

But VR can be a great attention-getter, a quick and easy way to create a sense of presence and place. By creating the impression of being somewhere, by giving the viewer the freedom to look up, down and all around, a lot of crucial contextual information can be derived that would, in more limited linear scenarios, require careful selection and plotting, only to wind up giving us the director's or writer's point of view.

Immersion can offer a counterweight to indifference. It can lure us into being interested in a topic we might otherwise gloss over, can encourage a search for facts, or a desire to learn. Rational debate, as a mode of discourse, is usually driven by some sort of motive. Immersion can help to create that motive, but – at least until we develop better ways of shaping and directing immersive experiences – it is not, in itself, a mode of discourse....

Emphasizing audience engagement poses its own issues, since news organizations have historically distinguished themselves from the commercial drivers that shape the rest of their network's operations, and journalists often resent the push to reach more viewers. At the same time, news organizations have seen their job as informing but not necessarily mobilizing the public, a goal more likely to be associated with documentary producers or activists. So, in what senses should journalists care about engagement?

The twentieth century is rich with embodiments of the journalistic profession, from news hounds, to crusaders, to hard-bitten cynics, to gonzo journalists, each articulating a different set of relations between journalists and their publics, as well as their larger institutional bases. And while it's probably true that many of today's practitioners hew to notions of independence, integrity, and authority that would be familiar to journalists of generations gone by, the increasingly dire conditions facing many American print organizations seem to be encouraging a more public-friendly stance.

I have the impression that many of the journalists who a few years back were forced to include their email address with their bylines and grudgingly cope with tweets are now more willing to interact with their public and to even track the number of hits their stories are getting.

News organizations, for all of their rhetoric about informing the public, not mobilizing it, also seem to be changing. This seems driven as much by the political polarization of the American public sphere as by charges from the political right that "the media" is too leftist, or by an outright political agenda on the part of some news organizations and funders (Fox News and Richard Mellon Scaife's *Pittsburgh Tribune-Review*, to name but two). That Fox News trademarked "Fair & Balanced" and "We Report. You Decide" as news slogans is one of the clearest signs that the old platitudes have been transformed into marketing tools, not commitments. Journalism – just like the larger environment it inhabits – is changing.

All that said, I think the engagement issue plays out on a somewhat different dimension. It's similar to what I said about immersive VR: it can help to generate interest, while making no claims to being a mode of discourse. First, it can indeed support the bottom line by attracting and holding readers and viewers. That's a double-edged sword, of course, as the annals of Yellow Journalism demonstrate. But the history of Pulitzer's *New York World* also shows that an engaged audience will stick with a paper even when the reporting improves! In other words, engagement is independent from journalistic quality in the traditional sense.

Second, engagement can be extensive. It can help to move people from an interest in the reports they read or see to the actual world and civic processes around them. If the journalistic information is solid, then whatever interventions follow will at least have the benefit of being well informed....

Engagement is user-centric. Rather than proclaiming from the lofty position of professional authority, it invites involvement, situates relevance, and demonstrates the need for further information and consideration.

Alas, the news no longer seems self-evident. Today's public faces a withering array of choices, a number of which pander shamelessly to their interests. It's an empowered public, which is not to say an informed one – a public with tools, access, and the means to express and share ideas. These developments are some of the reasons we believe that journalism is moving away from being a straightforward transmitter of information to a redefined position as a convener, curator, and shaper of an informed conversation between publics and sources. It's the difference between a monolog and a dialog. And today's public is increasingly part of the conversation ...

If a significant public does its reading and viewing on mobile devices, then we need to think about reaching them there, not simply by squeezing the printed page down to phone screen size, and not simply finding alternate ways to convey that information in small format. We also need to consider users' desires to navigate information, compare it, share it, and, at times, even produce it. We need to find a way to go beyond journalism as information transmission alone, and to think about ways of addressing its ritual dimensions, which I mentioned earlier when citing James Carey – and all this while somehow maintaining the reference values that quality journalism represents. No small challenge, but we've figured out the quality news and transmission bit, so the next step is to upgrade significantly the role of the user in our calculus.

News organizations and documentary producers struggle with the phenomenon of user-generated content. So-called "citizen journalists" are often pitted against professional news-gatherers and there's concerns that grassroots media may not meet the same standards of accuracy and ethics as those produced by professional journalists. Are there good ways for news organizations to collaborate with the public in order to expand their capacities without necessarily sacrificing older standards about quality reporting?

This picks up from the previous question, and it's the key issue in a change from monolog to dialog. What do we do with the conversation partner, especially when there are so few productive behavioral precedents available and even fewer ways to guarantee the quality of the conversation? Transitions are always vexed: how much of the old to retain? What of the new will actually stick? And, meanwhile, how are we supposed to navigate the uncertain mix of signals?

Recognizable standards and the ability to distinguish fact from fiction are more important than ever, particularly given the ever-growing cacophony of sources and voices enabled by our communication technologies. This is in part a literacy problem, in a world where diversity brings with it multiple and competing truths, and in part a curation problem, where reputation turns on appropriate and timely selection in a very chaotic information environment.

But the stakes are enormous in an environment that offers countless invitations for the public to share, and, in sharing, opportunities to build communities of interest and affiliation. These energies can be directed toward civic engagement and informed debate, or they can be siphoned off to support the narrow interests of closed communities. Journalism, at least in my view, should be a social binder ...

While the verdict is still out, there's no denying the role of the public in uploading information on events as they happen, and in commenting on, supplementing, and contesting journalistic reports, whether in the press or not. In really simplistic terms, on one hand, the public's contributions can be likened to sensory input, the raw data that something is happening that will quickly make its way to the brain for the dots to be connected. It's the nervous system at work, with a division of function that makes good use of both nerve ends and cognitive processing.

But on the other hand, public responses to published journalism (I learn a lot by reading the *Guardian*'s comments sections!) invoke a slightly different analogy. In this case, it's all at the processing level and similar to the internal debates we can have with ourselves. We reach a conclusion, but then consider the situation from different angles, or factor in different data points. These comments, if a civil tone can reign, go a long way toward improving journalism by offering contrasting views, linking to sources not mentioned in the original, and demonstrating the potentials of an incredibly productive partnership....

Reflections

My original comments were made in 2016, and, as with so much else in the American landscape, it's difficult to comprehend how much has changed in the intervening years. Mainstream news media, in particular, have been under sustained pressure, both economic and political. Falling circulation numbers, dropping advertisement revenues, closures, mergers, and more ... trends that in 2016 incentivized experimentation in new forms of news presentation have in some markets reached the point where they now inhibit innovation. So, too, the chilling effect brought about by the frontal assault on the news in the Trump era. Experimentation with collaborative news forms and interactive and immersive stories somehow seems less pressing at a moment when back-to-basics journalism promises a return to old certainties. The transmission of solid and well-researched facts seems to many news organizations like the best antidote to "fake news" – whether in the sense of purposefully corrupted information, or in the sense of reports that are disliked by the White House.

And yet James Carey's notion of *ritual*, of the sharing, exchanging, and participating fundamental to the communication process, has never seemed so important. Both sides of the political divide bond over the latest outrage, share evidence, and build narratives, drawing on presidential tweets, disaggregated Facebook articles, and scraps of speculation gleaned from cable news. And this notion of ritual, as I argued in 2016, is fundamental to the forms of collaboration and interactive configuration characteristic of the new documentary and its journalistic counterparts.

Lessons learned in the intervening years? Three stand out. First, ritual, like transmission, is a process that can work for good or ill, depending on how we deploy it. The transmission of corrupted content is as corrosive to the body politic as ritualistically enabled conspiracies. Form, in this sense, is neither cause nor symptom, but rather opportunity.

Second, as the various crises have mounted, some news organizations have retrenched to familiar ground, leaving forays into rituals of exchange and community-building to social media. Even the *Guardian*, one of the most experimental operations out there, has stopped running reader comments with its main news stories thanks to the disruptive behavior of ideologically motivated trolls. The transmission of well-researched news is vitally important, of course, but that shouldn't preclude embracing Carey's notion of communication rituals. Today's technologies and the robust examples offered by the documentary world show what is possible, and the terrain shouldn't be abandoned to the commercial interests of today's social media giants.

And there is a third compelling reason to consider, particularly, contributory and interactive models of documentary and journalism. Stories like the *Guardian*'s "The Counted" (a multi-year crowdsourced report on deaths in the US at the hands of the police) and the International Consortium of Investigative Journalists' posting of "The Panama Papers" (11.5 million leaked papers from the corporate service provider Mossack Fonseca) are beyond the scope of individual reporters and news organizations. They are sprawling data sets, require elaborate collaborations, and enable countless stories that emergent forms can do much to facilitate. The complexity and connectivity of today's world demand that we find better ways to collaborate and communicate, both effectively and affectively.

Notes

1 www.lutherblissett.net/archive/215_en.html
2 www.wumingfoundation.com/english/outtakes/whygiap.htm
3 https://iquindici.org
4 www.wheretheheckismatt.com
5 https://clalliance.org/blog/ifiasco-in-la-s-schools-why-technology-alone-is-never-the-answer
6 www.radiotopia.fm/showcase/ways-of-hearing
7 www.gameofphones.com
8 www.planetizen.com/node/34852
9 www.sciencedirect.com/science/article/pii/S0742051X17307898
10 www.jstor.org/stable/23269417?seq=1#page_scan_tab_contents
11 https://womensenews.org/2015/04/we-are-indias-daughter-and-change-is-our-name
12 www.youtube.com/watch?v=RZwM3GvaTRM
13 www.youtube.com/watch?v=HfuwNU0jsk0
14 www.youtube.com/watch?v=Gha3kEECqUk
15 www.youtube.com/watch?v=Gvj9ebIePIM
16 www.youtube.com/watch?v=5Z5ICVEIRIk
17 www.youtube.com/watch?v=X3-hOigoxHs
18 www.youtube.com/watch?v=C4kuR1gyOeQ

Index